Systematic Word Study

for Grade 1

An Easy Weekly Routine for Teaching Hundreds of New Words to Develop Strong Readers, Writers, & Spellers

Cheryl M. Sigmon

New York • Toronto • London • Auckland • Sydney
Mexico City • New Delhi • Hong Kong • Buenos Aires

Dedication

This book is dedicated to first-grade teachers
who give the gift of word knowledge to your students each and every day.

To my youngest grandson, Wake, who is learning the power of words
from his parents, grandparents, and teachers. Your words bring great joy to my life!

And, as always, to my husband, Ray, whose patience and support
during my writing is amazing!

And, heartfelt thanks to my editor, Joanna Davis-Swing.
Your careful eye, immeasurable patience, depth of knowledge,
and gentle spirit have guided me every step of the way.
This is, no doubt, a far better resource because of you!

Cover design by Jaime Lucero
Cover photograph by Getty Images/Fuse
Interior design by Sarah Morrow
Editor: Joanna Davis-Swing
Copy Editor: Jeannie Hutchins

ISBN: 978-0-545-24159-5
Copyright © 2011 Cheryl M. Sigmon
All rights reserved.
Printed in the U.S.A.

1 2 3 4 5 6 7 8 9 10   40   16 15 14 13 12 11

Contents

How Literacy Grows in the First-Grade Classroom

Of all the years that comprise a child's educational career, first grade may be the most magical one of all. It is the year that children may be most eager to learn, the year that they are most curious about everything in the world around them, and the year they grow by leaps and bounds socially, emotionally, and academically, especially in language and literacy.

Entering first grade with limited reading and writing skills and varying experiences with books, six-year-olds grow exponentially as they are exposed to the most basic literacy concepts. What they hear, what we read to them, what we write for them, what they attempt to read and write, and the word-rich environments we create in our classrooms and schools combine to transform these children. Wise teachers carefully structure their day to foster literacy growth, infusing literacy learning into every experience. As we peek into a classroom, we'll get a taste of this thoughtful planning that reaps great literacy rewards.

Literacy Learning in Action: Morning Message

The day begins with "carpet chatter" time when all children sit crossed-legged on the carpet in a cozy spot in the classroom. After a few activities, including a morning song and several show-and-tell presentations, the teacher writes a morning message on chart paper:

> *Dear Class,*
>
> *Today we will learn many new things. We are looking for clues that autumn is here. We will write and read about autumn. We will go to art to make leaf rubbings. Let's get started with our day!*
>
> *Love,*
> *Miss Truluck*

Systematic Word Study for Grade 1 © 2011 by Cheryl M. Sigmon, Scholastic Teaching Resources

The class reads the morning message together as the teacher taps each word with her pointer. They take the time to count the sentences, distinguishing them from the number of lines in the message. The teacher writes "5 sentences" at the top of the chart. They count the number of letters in a few of the words like *learn, today,* and *autumn* and write the totals above the words. They search for some of the high-frequency words they've been studying, underlining them and reading them aloud. The teacher stresses how important these words are because they will help them to read and write easily. They discuss why capitals are needed at the beginnings of sentences and names like Miss Truluck. Also, they look at a new end punctuation mark "!" and think about why it is used instead of a period.

In just a few minutes, this teacher has done some powerful literacy work with her children. First, by writing a letter to the class, she modeled how words are used to communicate ideas. By counting the sentences and the letters in some words, she has distinguished letters from words and reinforced the idea that sentences are made up of groups of words. With a pointer, she has demonstrated the one-to-one correspondence between spoken and written language—not always an easy connection for children to make and an essential print concept. In looking for high-frequency words, which always appear in such messages, she has emphasized how knowing such words builds fluency in reading and writing.

In first grade, the exploration of letters and words in all sorts of contexts—such as a Morning Message—provides the basic print and language concepts that our students need. We want our children to understand that sounds are represented by symbols called letters, and that those letters combine to make units called words, and those words link to make sentences that express our thoughts and feelings or that allow us to discover the thoughts and feelings of others. We want to give our children the words they need to express themselves and to understand the world around them. And we want to give our children the tools they need to become successful readers and writers. That's why word study is so essential in first grade.

A Focus on Word Study

Word study is an integral part of any literacy program, and the exploration of letters and sounds, words and word parts, is embedded throughout the school day. However, it is important to reserve time regularly for a focused, systematic study of phonemic awareness, phonics, alphabetic principles, and basic print concepts. At the same time, we can build students' vocabulary as we explore new words and engage in word play. Fun and fast-paced lessons can help solidify children's knowledge about words and sound-spelling relationships.

The failure to place proper emphasis on word knowledge can have devastating consequences for reading. For example, we know that the absence of adequate word knowledge disrupts fluency and directly impairs reading comprehension. In fact, word meaning makes up as much as 70-80% of comprehension (Pressley, 2002). So, we provide a word study time in our curriculum, in part, to improve reading comprehension.

For these reasons, we need to value and include word study in our daily instructional program, beginning as soon as students enter school. The lessons in this book are designed to help you as you nurture and support students' growth in language and literacy; the fast-paced, engaging activities complement the literacy work you do throughout the day.

The Words We Teach

The Power of High-Frequency Words

Certain words in our written and spoken English language are, of necessity, repeated frequently. In fact, three little words—*I, and, the*—account for 10% of all printed words! The top 25 words account for one-third of all print. And, amazingly, 100 of the top high-frequency words account for half of all printed text (Zeno, Ivens, Millard, & Duvvuri, 1995). However, many of the high-frequency words pose difficulties for our students because they tend to be abstract and have irregular spellings.

Building automaticity, or quickness, with high-frequency words means that the reader does not have to stop and consciously labor over decoding them. Our goal, even with the simple high-frequency words, is not merely to have the students memorize the words for a test on Friday, but rather to have students know these words automatically for the long term. This automaticity comes only through repetition and multi-sensory engagement with the words and features of the words. And, you will see that the activities in these lessons do just that—engage each and every learner!

In this book, you will find many high-frequency words selected from kindergarten and first grade high-frequency lists, along with some second-grade words. For some children, a number of the words will serve as review; for others, they may be new words that are necessary for fluency building. Many teachers who take only a cursory look at these lessons heavily laden with one and two syllable words may ask—*How can these lessons be multi-level enough to address the needs of all of my learners from the lowest to the highest achievers? Do the lessons provide enough of a challenge for those students who could certainly be learning words far more difficult and multisyllabic?*

To answer these questions, I invite you to look closely at what is embedded in the lessons. In each lesson, students explore a range of literacy elements from the basic alphabetic principles of letter and sound identification to the more advanced skills of sorting, analyzing features, and using analogy. Some of the words involved in the activities may even be difficult for some of your students, but those segments of the lessons are brief enough to challenge those who are ready without diminishing the interest and motivation of others who are not quite ready for that challenge.

Including Content Vocabulary and General Academic Vocabulary

Some critical content and general academic vocabulary words are included in almost all of the 35 lessons. While they do not include all content and academic words that your students need to know, they do represent major concepts in first grade and are used across the content areas in classroom talk. Being alongside more familiar high-frequency words in these lessons allows you to present them in a less intimidating manner than they might appear in a textbook. These words are analyzed just as the high-frequency words are, but they allow for exploration of multisyllabic words and key concepts.

The content areas represented are math, science, social studies, language arts, and art. Additionally, a few character education words are included, such as *thank you* and *please* and some that allow for further discussion about character building such as *hero* and *honor*. The correct spellings of these words, many of which are big words that might be difficult for some of your students, are not as important at this level as spellings of the high-frequency words.

Introducing Basic Print and Language Concepts

The first five weeks of lessons in this book provide a foundation in print and language concepts. With the daily lessons and guided practice, students will develop the following understandings:

- Words are made of individual letters.
- Letters represent certain sounds.
- Written words and spoken language have a direct match.
- Words link to make sentences.
- Sentences make sense and express complete thoughts.
- We read from left to right.
- Sentences end with punctuation.
- Some words sound alike (rhyme).
- Some words share spelling patterns (rimes).
- Spelling patterns of some words help us to read and write many other words.
- We can manipulate letters and sounds to create new words.
- Words have beats or syllables.
- Some letters are called vowels and some are consonants.

These simple lessons have a big impact right from the beginning. You will teach word knowledge that empowers students in their wider grasp and use of words—far beyond the immediate lesson.

The lessons beyond week five reinforce these basic concepts. The dictation writing and sentence-building activities are dropped in favor of more in-depth analysis of the words on the list. After week five, each child is responsible for manipulating his or her own words and letters in response to your questions and directions. There will be a higher skill level and understanding necessary to complete these tasks, although the lessons remain multi-level. You will still ask students to point to letters that represent certain sounds, but you will also ask what words are made if certain letters are replaced. There is also great emphasis placed on rime patterns in these exercises, since rimes enable children to read and write many additional words with the same patterns. You will also familiarize students with the concept that often a particular sound pattern may have different spelling patterns. Awareness of that concept is all that is important at this level—students don't need to be able to spell all of the different patterns that make a certain sound.

Lessons become appropriately more challenging but continue to remain multi-level to meet the needs of all of your students. The chart on pages 8–11 summarizes the words and skills taught each week.

First Grade Word Chart

Week	High-Frequency Words	Content Words	Main Words From Secondary Activities	Important Word Features
1	an, am, man, me, name, same	Social Studies (me, man, name)	men, names, fan, pan, tan, ran, van	basic print and language concepts; plurals formed in different ways; rhyming words; pronouns; suffixes; long-*a* sound; rime patterns: *-ame, -an, -am*; Word Builder: *names*
2	in, win, wing, king, walk, walking	Social Studies (king)	win, kin, ink, link, wink, wing, king, din, fin, pin, tin	basic print and language concepts; rhyming words; suffixes; rime patterns: *-ing, -in, -ink*; Word Builder: *walking*
3	at, sat, let, met, tall, small	Math (small, tall)	mat, set, all, mall, smallest, bat, cat, fat, hat, pat, rat, vat	basic print and language concepts; rhyming words; short-*a*; superlatives (small, smaller, smallest); rime patterns: *-at, -et, -all*; Word Builder: *smallest*
4	in, pin, tap, tan, pan, paint	Art (paint)	tin, nap, pain, cap, gap, lap, map, rap, sap, zap	basic print and language concepts; rime patterns: *-in, -an, -ap*; short-*i*; plurals by adding *-s*; synonyms; Word Builder: *paint*
5	is, it, get, set, rest, tiger	Math (set)	sit, sir, stir, tire, tigers, pit, bit, fit, hit, kit, lit, wit	basic print and language concepts; syllabication; rime patterns: *-est, -et, -ir, -it*; plurals; multiple meaning words; Word Builder: *tigers*
6	they, please, saw, pretty, went, want	Character word (please)	set, pet, net, ten, pen, pest, nest, sent, spent	primer review words; syllabication; onset blends *pl-, pr-*; rime patterns: *-aw, -et, -en, -ent, -est*; pronouns; long-*e* sound; Word Builder: *spent*
7	jump, who, help, after, well, our	Character word (help); General Academic Vocabulary (who)	fan, tan, ran, fat, rat, ear, near, fear, tear, afternoon	primer review words; syllabication; pronouns; rime patterns: *-an, -at, -ear*; Word Builder: *afternoon*
8	brown, not, at, what, get, good, there	Character word (good); General Academic Vocabulary (what); Art (brown)	top, sop, stop, dot, tot pot, spot, spotted	some primer words; rime patterns: *-at, -ar, -op, -ot, -et*; onset blend *wh-, th-, br-*; Word Builder: *spotted*
9	thank, some, stop, had, his, her	Character word (thank)	at, hat, fat, flat, hut, hunt, hunk, tank, thankful	primer words; rime patterns: *-at, -ank*; onset blends: *st-, th-*; Word Builder: *thankful*
10	under, black, white, must, say, soon	Art (black, white)	den, hen, ten, then, run, runt, hunt, hunted, thunder	primer words; syllabication; rime patterns: *-en, -unt, -ust, -ack, -ay*; onset blends: *bl-, wh-*; Word Builder: *thunder*

Systematic Word Study for Grade 1 © 2011 by Cheryl M. Sigmon, Scholastic Teaching Resources

Week	High-Frequency Words	Content Words	Main Words From Secondary Activities	Important Word Features
11	down, where, funny, that, out, into	General Academic Vocabulary (where)	in, tin, tins, ice, nice, cent, cents, insect, insects	plurals; opposites; syllabication; different spellings for same sound; rime patterns: *-in, -ice, -own, -out, -at*; onset blend: *wh-*; Word Builder: *insects*
12	said, little, play	Social Studies (city, citizen, state)	pet, met, let, lap, tap, map, ate, mate, late, plate, lay, may, pay, play, playmate	compound words; syllabication; different spellings for same sound; multiple meaning words; rime patterns: *-et, -ap, -ate, -ay*; Word Builder: *playmate*
13	then, when, I	Math (minute, month, total) General Academic Vocabulary (when)	in, tin, sin, me, met, set, net, nets, nut, nuts, must, men, menu, menus, minute, minutes	pronoun; capitalization (pronoun *I*); syllabication; plurals; rime patterns: *-in, -en, -et*; Word Builder: *minutes*
14	you, too, red, look, how, year	Art (red); Math (year)	car, care, dare, can, ran, and, land, lane, cane, end, lend, race, calendar	primer words; homophones; pronouns; rime patterns: *-ook, -ed, -ear, -end, -an, -and, -are, -ane*; Word Builder: *calendar*
15	we, for, can't, down, come	Science (light)	me, met, pet, up, cup, cop, top, mop, rot, cot, pot, put, cute, mute, tore, more, core, come, computer	primer words; contractions; rime patterns: *-own, -e, -ight, -et, -up, -ot, -op, -ute, -ore*; Word Builder: *computer*
16	up, see, my, yellow, on	Language Arts/ Math/General Academic Vocabulary (question); Art (yellow)	in, tin, ten, it, sit, quit, son, ton, tons, tune, tunes, toe, toes, nose, nest, nests, quest, question, questions	primer words; plurals formed by adding *-s*; syllabication; rime patterns: *-in, -it, -est, -on, -tion, -y, -ee, -up*; spelling pair: *qu-*; Word Builder: *questions*
17	go, do, one, big	Science (plant, planet)	an, ran, sag, nag, rag, snag, rang, sang, gas, dear, dare, red, read, end, send, grand, gardens	primer words; syllabication; homophones; multiple meaning words; onset blend: *pl-*; rime patterns: *-an, -ag, -ang, -end, -ig*; Word Builder: *gardens*
18	make, away, blue, here, think	Art (blue); Math and General Academic Vocabulary (unit, think)	it, sit, pit, pits, spit, sip, tip, tips, pie, pies, up, cup, cups, put, cut, cute, cuter, tire, tires, site, spite, sprite, picture, pictures	primer words; syllabication; homophones; different spellings for same sound; onset blends: *bl-, th-*; rime patterns: *-it, -ip, -ite, -ink, -ake*; Word Builder: *pictures*
19	run, find, three, from	Math (skip, odd, three); General Academic (find)	in, ding, ring, rang, are, dare, age, rage, rag, nag, ran, range, danger, grade, garden, red, read, reading	primer words; multiple meaning words; homophones; onset blends: *fr-, sk-, thr-*; rime patterns: *-ing, -age, -ag, -ind, -ip*; Word Builder: *reading*

Week	High-Frequency Words	Content Words	Main Words From Secondary Activities	Important Word Features
20	but, with, this, has, again	Social Studies (future)	at, hat, sat, rat, shy, dry, try, day, hay, ray, say, stay, stray, tray, dust, dusty, rust, rusty, Thursday	primer words; syllabication; capitalization of days of week; rime patterns: -at, -ay, -ust; Word Builder: *Thursday*
21	will, did, so, no	Social Studies (vote, election)	lie, tie, let, net, set, ice, lice, nice, slice, cone, lone, tone, stone, elect	primer words; syllabication; homophones; rime patterns: -ice, -o, -et, -ie, id, -ill, -one; Word Builder: *elections*
22	like, yes, four, me, fly	Science (weather, fly)	an, ran, tan, man, met, net, wet, where, when, art, mart, tart, eat, ate, name, tame, math, earth, weatherman	primer words; question words (what, where, when); syllabication; Tense (*ate/eat*); compound words; rime patterns: -an, -e, -et, -ike, -art, -ame, -y; Word Builder: *weatherman*
23	now, new, to, ran	Social Studies (past, present)	at, sat, rat, art, dart, day, say, ray, dry, try, rust, dust, rusty, dusty, Saturday	primer words; syllabication; homophones; capitalizing proper nouns and days of week; rime patterns: -at, -an, -ow, -ew, -art, -ay, -ust, -usty, -y; Word Builder: *Saturday*
24	eat, ate, him, could	Science (heat, freezing)	ad, dad, sad, send, and, sand, need, seed, weed, day, way, say, sway, saw, new, news, swan, Wednesday	primer words; syllabication; tense *eat/ate*; capitalizing proper nouns; rime patterns: -ate, -eat, -ad, -end, -and, -eed, -ay, -ould; Word Builder: *Wednesday*
25	ask, of, open, much	Social Studies/ Character (hero, honor); General Academic Vocabulary (ask)	tan, ran, van, vans, vest, rest, nest, ear, vent, sent, rent, save, rave, veteran, veterans	primer words; syllabication; blend: *sk*; forming plural with -s; rime patterns: -ask, -at, -an, -est, -ear, -ent, -ave; Word Builder: *veterans*
26	as, them, many, would	Language Arts / Character (character, setting); General Academic Vocabulary (would)	car, tar, star, scar, rest, chest, art, cart, chart, characters	some second-grade words; syllabication; rime patterns: -ould, -ing, -ar, -est, -art; Word Builder: *characters*
27	over, any, know, don't	Science (insect, cycle)	hope, rope, hop, shop, shops, he, she, rap, gap, sap, rag, sag, grass, grasshopper	some second-grade words; syllabication; multiple meaning words; contractions; pronouns; rime patterns: -ope, -op, -e, -ap, -ag; Word Builder: *grasshopper*
28	just, take, may, before	Math (length, half)	sun, run, gun, rug, mug, snug, smug, game, same, name, ring, sing, rain, main, gain, measuring	some second-grade words; multiple meaning words; syllabication; rime patterns: -un, -ug, -ame, -ing, -ain, -ust, -ake, -ay; Word Builder: *measuring*

Systematic Word Study for Grade 1 © 2011 by Cheryl M. Sigmon, Scholastic Teaching Resources

Week	High-Frequency Words	Content Words	Main Words From Secondary Activities	Important Word Features
29	out, old, going, always	Social Studies (continent, country)	in, tin, sin, not, cot, cent, sent, tent, nest, test, contest, continent, continents	some second-grade words; syllabication; different spellings for same sound; multisyllabic word; rime patterns: -out, -old, -in, -ot, -est, -ent; Word Builder: *continents*
30	every, again, very	Language Arts and General Academic Vocabulary (information, predict, vowel)	in, fin, tin, moon, noon, arm, farm, far, tar, form, inform, information	some second-grade words; syllabication; different spellings for same sound; multisyllabic words; rime patterns: -in, -oon, -arm, -ar; Word Builder: *information*
31	walk, give, which	Science (invent, matter, classify; General Academic Vocabulary (which)	vine, nine, nest, vest, ten, tens, tennis, vote, vet, vets, tennis, vote, vet, vets, sent, vent, invent, inventions	some second-grade words; syllabication; multisyllabic words; multiple meaning words; rime patterns: -alk, -ive, -ine, -est, -ent; Word Builder: *inventions*
32	round, live, fast	Language Arts (fantasy, reality, fiction); Math (round)	it, fit, sit, set, yet, ray, say, stay, lay, relay, layer, flat, slat, reality, fair, fairly, fairy, fairy tales	some second-grade words; syllabication; multisyllabic words; suffixes: -er, -ly, -ty; rime patterns: -ive, -ound, -it, -et, -ay, -at; Word Builder: *fairy tales*
33	once, your, you're	Math (vertical, horizontal, greater)	fly, sly, elf, self, or, for, fore, lore, sore, our, flour, your, yourself	some second-grade words; syllabication; multisyllabic words; homophones; superlatives; compound words; -gh and -ph as /f/; rime patterns: -y, -elf, -ore, -our; Word Builder: *yourself*
34	their, put	Math (enough, graph, chart, solve)	pop, top, hop, stop, pot, got, hot, shot, spot, port, sport, sap, gap, graphs, photo, photos, photographs	some second-grade words; homophones; pronouns; multisyllabic words; syllabication; plurals formed with -s; rime patterns: -op, -ot, -art, -ort, -ap; Word Builder: *photographs*
35	because, where, were	Science (machine, environment, shelter); General Academic Vocabulary (where)	at, hat, that, sat, bat, bath, it, its, sit, hit, bit, tab, stab, habit, habitat, habitats	some second-grade words; syllabication; synonyms; onset blends: sh-, wh-; suffix: -ment; rime patterns: -at, -it, -ab; Word Builder: *habitats*

Weekly Activities: The Why's and How-to's

The five-day plan for each of 35 weeks throughout the year provides many opportunities for your students to explore how words work. Further, the lessons also provide hands-on, explicit instruction in most, if not all, of the word level state standards I reviewed when compiling this book and creating its activities.

Lessons 1-5

This series of lessons is designed to introduce your students to the basic print and language concepts that they need to grow as readers and writers. For the first five weeks, they are prescribed daily to help students become familiar with the word study routines and develop some basic letter and word knowledge. After week five, there is more variety to the lessons, which helps sustain motivation and engagement.

At the beginning of the week, make a class set of the Word Card Template for that week's lesson—one copy per student. You may also want to write the words and letters on index cards so you can display them in a pocket chart. Then work through the following lesson sequence, one lesson per day.

Day 1: Word Builder

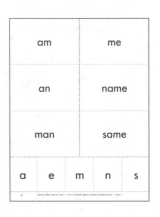

This activity teaches the following concepts:

- Words are made of letters.
- Letters represent sounds.
- Some words sound alike—rhyme
- Some words have useful spelling patterns (rimes) that help spell other words.
- We can manipulate letters and sounds to create new words.

Preparation: Cut along the horizontal line on the bottom of the Word Card Template to separate the letter strip from the words. You can cut apart the letters and place them in a seal-top plastic bag to hand out to students, or you may distribute the bags and letter strips and have students tear apart the letters. Reserve the rest of the Word Card Template for use on Day 5.

Directions: Students use the letters to build words, following your directions. This activity helps students see how letters and sounds can be manipulated to form different words and builds an awareness of spelling patterns.

Provide as much guidance as your particular students need. If you notice students have difficulty with a task—such as finding two letters to spell *at*—ask for an oral response first. If that's not enough support, model the task for them on the board or with a pocket chart. As students gain greater understanding about sounds and letters, you can reduce the level of support. Occasionally, you might offer hints such as, "Now keep the same letters and find one letter to add to *an* to spell the word *man*."

When you've finished with the activity, have students put the letters in the plastic bag and store them for later use.

Day 2: Dictation

This activity teaches the following concepts:

- Sentences express a complete thought.
- Sentences are made of words.

Systematic Word Study for Grade 1 © 2011 by Cheryl M. Sigmon, Scholastic Teaching Resources

- Words are made of letters.
- Sentences start with capital letters.
- Sentences end with punctuation marks.
- Print moves from left to right.

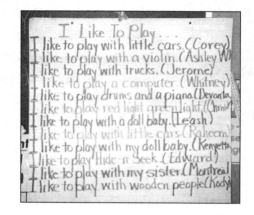

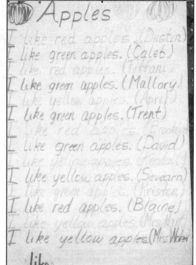

Preparation: Write the day's sentence frame on chart paper, writing the sentence for each student in your class to complete, plus an extra sentence to serve as the model (so if you have 24 students, write the sentence frame 25 times).

Directions: The sentence frame relates to the big word from the Day 1 Word Builder activity. Read the sentence frame aloud and fill in the blank in the first line with a word of your choice. Discuss the sentence, then invite each student to provide a word that completes the sentence frame sensibly. Write the word(s) in the blank to model letter formation and keep the lesson moving; you may want to write each child's name after his or her sentence to identify them. Keep the chart handy; it is used in the Day 3 lesson.

Day 3: Sentence Builder

This activity teaches the following concepts:

- Sentences express a complete thought.
- Sentences start with capital letters.
- Spoken words match printed words.
- Sentences are made of words.
- Sentences end with punctuation marks.
- Print moves from left to right.

Preparation: Choose three sentences students created for the Day 2 chart. Write each on a separate sentence strip. Have the chart available.

Directions: Begin the activity by having each student come to the chart and read the sentence he or she dictated, using a pointer to tap each word as it is read. If students are having trouble with one-to-one correspondence (tapping a word as they say it), place your hand over theirs and guide the pointer.

After each student has read his or her sentence, seat them all. Take the first sentence strip you prepared, acknowledge whose sentence it is, and read the sentence aloud, pointing to each word as you go. Then take your scissors and cut it apart, word by word, so students see that sentences are made up of individual words. Pass out

the words to several students, giving the student-contributed word to the student who dictated the sentence. Ask these students to come to the front of the class and arrange themselves in order of the sentence from left to right, offering assistance as necessary. With these students facing the class, walk behind each as they hold up their word and ask that the class read the sentence together aloud.

Repeat this procedure with the two remaining sentence strips you have prepared.

Day 4: Rhymer

This activity teaches the following concepts:

- Words are made of letters.
- Letters represent sounds.
- Some words sound alike—rhyme.
- Some words have useful spelling patterns (rimes) that help spell other words.
- Text can be supported by pictures.
- We can manipulate letters and sounds to create new words.

Materials: letters from letter strip distributed in Day 1; board or chart paper; art paper for each student (optional)

Directions: Follow directions provided in the lesson, which guide students to use the analogy strategy to read and write new words. Having students illustrate the rhyming words is optional; however, it provides another dimension to the multi-sensory experience that can help them process the words and patterns.

Day 5: Word Smart

This activity teaches the following concepts:

- Words are made of letters.
- Sounds are represented by certain letters.
- Some words sound alike—rhyme.
- We can manipulate letters and sounds to create new words.
- Words have meaning.
- Some letters go above and some go below the line.
- Some words have the same meanings and some have opposite meanings—synonyms and antonyms.
- Some words add an "s" to mean more than one.

Preparation: Prepare the Word Card Template as follows:

- Place several copies together, fold the copies along the mid-page vertical line, keeping the words to the outside.
- From the outside edges of the paper, cut towards the folded edge and stop within a half-inch of the fold. Do this for each of the words.

Systematic Word Study for Grade 1 © 2011 by Cheryl M. Sigmon, Scholastic Teaching Resources

- Unfold the copies, keeping them together, and cut from the bottom middle of the paper straight up the dotted vertical line to within an inch of the top.
- The papers should faintly resemble a rib cage and will stay intact as you pass them out to the students.

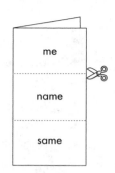

Directions: Distribute the Word Card Templates to students and direct them to detach the words quickly by pulling them apart. Encourage them not to attempt to tear perfectly as you want this accomplished quickly. Ask students to spread the six words across the top of their desks or tables with the words facing up. This will also provide generous work space for them, which will keep little elbows from knocking words on the floor. As you ask questions, ask students to respond in one of these ways:

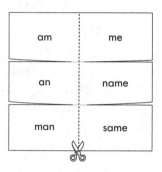

- Search for the answers among the six words. Pick up the word or words that answer the question and hold it for you to see. If there are more than two correct answers, just use two answers. (Don't be alarmed that some students get their answers from what their friends are displaying. Apparently, they need that support, and this will help them.)
- Search for the answers among the six words. Move the word or words that answer the question to the workspace for you to check as you monitor the room.

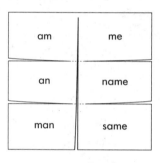

Ask the questions and affirm responses at the pace you deem appropriate for your students. Praise their efforts liberally!

At the end of the lesson, have students place the word cards in the bags with the letters, and send the materials home for them to practice.

Lessons 6-35

Starting in week 6, you will have choices to make about the activities you feel might best engage your students. Some of the activities are consistent across the weeks, such as the Day 1: Meet the Words. Students need this hands-on introduction to each word. On Days 2 and 3, however, you can choose activities from the Free Choice options on pages 18–20.

As in the first five weeks, begin by preparing copies of the week's Word Card Template.

Day 1: Meet the Words

In addition to providing practice reading the week's words, this activity teaches the following concepts:

- Words are made of letters.
- Sounds are represented by certain letters.
- Words have distinguishing features.
- Some letter clusters make sounds different from the single letters in that cluster.
- Some words have other words in them.
- Words have syllables.

- Some words sound like other words—rhyme.
- Some words have multiple meanings.
- Some words have spelling patterns that help to spell other words.
- Some words sound alike but have different spelling patterns and meanings.
- Some letters are consonants and some are vowels.
- We don't always hear every letter in a word.
- Some letters go above and some below the line.
- Words have meanings.

Preparation: Prepare the Word Card Template as described on page 14.

- Place several copies together, fold the copies along the mid-page vertical line, keeping the words to the outside.
- From the outside edges of the paper, cut towards the folded edge and stop within a half-inch of the fold. Do this for each of the words.
- Unfold the copies, keeping them together, and cut from the bottom middle of the paper straight up the dotted vertical line to within an inch of the top.
- The papers should faintly resemble a rib cage and will stay intact as you pass them out to the students.

Directions: Distribute the Word Card Templates and small plastic bags to students. Direct them to detach the words quickly by pulling them apart. Encourage them not to attempt to tear with perfection as you want this accomplished quickly. Ask students to spread the six words across the top of their desks or tables with the words facing up. This will also provide generous work space for them, which will keep little elbows from knocking words on the floor. As you ask questions, ask students to respond in one of these ways:

- Search for the answers among the six words. Pick up the word or words that answer the question and hold it for you to see. If there are more than two correct answers, just use two answers. (Don't be alarmed that some students get their answers from what their friends are displaying. Apparently, they need that support, and this will help them.)
- Search for the answers among the six words. Move the word or words that answer the question to the workspace for you to check as you monitor the room.

Ask the questions and affirm responses at the pace you deem appropriate for your students. Praise their efforts liberally!

At the end of the lesson, have students place the word cards in the bags and store for later use.

Day 2: Word Whittle

Word Whittle teaches all of the same concepts listed in Meet the Words, and it also helps them learn to categorize words by their features

Materials: Word cards from Day 1 activity

Directions: Ask students to spread the words out across the top of their desks so that there is adequate workspace. You will read a series of questions; after each one, students select the words

Systematic Word Study for Grade 1 © 2011 by Cheryl M. Sigmon, Scholastic Teaching Resources

that fit. For example, you might ask students to find the words that begin with the letter *m*; they would choose all words from that week that begin with *m*. For each subsequent question in the set, students choose from their "whittled" selections, returning the ones that do not fit to the top of their work space. No new words can be added to the group after the first question is read. After the final question in a set, only one word will remain. Students return it to the top of their work space before the next set of questions is given.

If time allows, choose an activity from the options on pages 18–20.

Day 3: Free Choice

On this day, choose one or two Free Choice activities from pages 18–20, based on the time available and the experiences you feel would help your students.

Day 4: Word Builder

In addition to exposing students to many new words, this activity teaches the following concepts:

- Words are made of letters.
- Letters represent sounds.
- Some words sound alike—rhyme.
- Some words have useful spelling patterns (rimes) that help spell other words.
- We can manipulate letters and sounds to create new words.
- Some words sound alike but have different spelling patterns.

Materials: Use the letter strips that you detached from the Word Card Template on Day 1. You may either cut them apart and distribute to students, or distribute them and have students tear them apart carefully.

Directions: Students use the letters to build words, following your directions. This activity helps students see how letters and sounds can be manipulated to form different words and builds an awareness of spelling patterns.

Ultimately, all of the letters will be used to build the big mystery word. Feel free to adapt the lesson for your students; you may choose to leave out some words, and in later lessons—where the number of words made increases—I shade words to indicate they are optional. Just be sure to include the words that contain the spelling pattern(s) you will use in the second part of the lesson, where students sort words and generate rhyming words.

When you've finished with the activity, have students put the letters in the plastic bag and store them for later use.

Day 5: Word Smart

This activity reinforces all of the same concepts and word features listed in Meet the Words. It is the same activity students are familiar with from the first five weeks; use the same directions as given on page 14.

Homework

At the end of the week, send home the letters and word cards in the plastic bags they have been stored in. Students can practice making words and reading the words; parents can join in to extend the practice. (See the letter on page 127 that goes home to parents at the beginning of the year to explain the types of activities they can do with their children.) You may also want to send home an activity record sheet (see page 128) that parents can fill out and send back in.

The take-home materials encourage and foster:

- A school to home connection
- Independence in word study
- Manipulation of letters/sounds to form new words
- Practice with phonics and phonemic awareness

Free Choice Lessons

Word Match

This activity gives students a fun way to practice reading the week's words. It also builds visual memory and word recognition.

Materials: Word cards

Directions: Place students in pairs. Have partners mix all of their cards together face down on a work space. Then they take turns turning over two cards at a time to make a matching pair. A student must read both words turned over; if they match, the student collects the cards, and the partner takes a turn. The student with the most cards collected when the teacher calls time wins this game. At the end of the game, have students separate the words so each has a complete set and store them in the small plastic bags.

Word Pop

This activity teaches word identification through multisensory engagement.

Materials: Word cards

Directions: Students turn all six word cards face down on their desks. Then they randomly turn over any two words. Call out a word. If students have that word face up, they "pop up," saying the word and showing it to the class. The students can choose two new words to turn over after a couple of rounds.

Word Swat

This activity teaches rapid word identification through multisensory engagement and provides an opportunity to review words from previous weeks.

Materials: board or two sheets of poster board; two fly swatters

Directions: On separate ends of the board or on two posters (see directions below), write the six new words for the week along with 6-12 words from previous weeks. Duplicate the list on both sides

Systematic Word Study for Grade 1 © 2011 by Cheryl M. Sigmon, Scholastic Teaching Resources

of the board or on the two posters, although you do not need to put the words in the same order. Divide the students into two teams, and line up each team in front of the word list on either side of the board or in front of the posters. Give a fly swatter to each of the children at the front of the line. Call out a word. The first child to locate and swat the correct word earns a point for that team and then goes to the end of the line. This repeats with each child and can continue as long as time allows. The team with the most points wins the challenge.

Extend the activity by giving extra points if students can use the word in a sentence or can share a word that rhymes. This is also a great activity for reviewing math facts and content vocabulary words and definitions.

Tips on Constructing the Posters

Use two full-sized sheets of poster board. Make 40 cutouts using a dye-cut machine, or purchase sticky-notes in shapes from your local dollar store. Choose a light or bright color over which a marker can be seen. Glue 20 shapes on each of the posters in random fashion. Laminate both posters. Each time you use this activity, use a water based transparency marker to write the words you want to review with your students over each of the shapes. After the activity, you can easily erase the poster for future use. Before erasing them, you might choose to use them in the literacy center for students to practice calling out and swatting the words.

Word Sort

This activity teaches students to categorize words based on features such as number of syllables, number of letters, spelling patterns, or other elements. It also helps them develop an understanding of the relationships between certain words.

Materials: Word cards

Directions: In each weekly lesson, I list the common features of the week's words in Day 3, the Free Choice Activity day. Simply call out a feature—such as words with one syllable—and ask students to find all words with that feature and put them in their workspace. You might ask them to check with a buddy to see if everyone agrees before you confirm the correct answers and discuss them.

Voice Choice

This activity teaches word identification and helps students explore the connotations of words.

Materials: Word cards

Directions: Choose a familiar character, and invite students to say and spell all of the week's words in the voice of that character. For example, you might choose a pirate, a tiger, a singer, a robot, a duck, a cheerleader, a teacher, and so on. Just have fun with this one!

Cheer the Words

This activity helps students remember the spelling of words and gets them actively engaged in learning!

Directions: Chant the words and their spellings like a cheer and allow some of the movements of cheerleading. Cheering and chanting the words several times can help students commit the spellings to memory. This one can help you all get some exercise as well as learning the words!

Word Detective

This activity develops students' word identification skills and helps them recognize words in context.

Directions: Give students a defined amount of time to look for this week's words in text and/or in their environment. They may enjoy this task more if they work with a partner or small group.

Rhymer

See description and directions on page 14.

Maximizing the Impact of Your Lessons

Here are some hints that will help you make the most of these lessons:

- Be sure that *every* student participates in these lessons. All students should have the opportunity to manipulate their own letters and words in response to your guidance. Remember that the lessons are multilevel, in order to address the individual needs of a range of achievement levels. So, when some students struggle a bit with parts of a lesson, be sure to offer the support they need to be successful.

- All teachers have to deal with short weeks from time to time, so here's a recommended plan for the number of days you might have:

3-Day Plan:

Day 1: Introduce the Words

Day 2: Word Builder

Day 3: Word Smart

4-Day Plan:

Day 1: Introduce the Words

Day 2: Choice Options (1 or 2)

Day 3: Word Builder

Day 4: Word Smart

- Involve parents in this word study plan. Take advantage of open-house nights or conferences to explain how they can support your efforts in building their child's word knowledge. At the conclusion of the weekly activities, send home the seal-top plastic bag of letters and words that you've used during the week. Include a Parent-Child Word Work homework activity sheet (see page 128). Be sure to fill in the blanks with spelling patterns and high-frequency words from the week. Everything else on the sheet will be completed by the parents/students.

- Briskly pace all the activities in your weekly plan. Reassure students who are struggling that they'll soon catch up. The activities are constructed to be multileveled so that they are appropriate for low-achieving, average, and high-achieving students. For example, Word Builder starts with simple two-letter words and works up to the mystery word, which is usually multisyllabic. Not all students will be able to build the mystery word before they see you write it.

- Go beyond these lessons with your instruction and exploration. You must still teach vocabulary in your reading and content lessons; however, as your students analyze the words through these systematic lessons, they should develop word savvy that transfers as they encounter the words in other contexts.

Systematic Word Study for Grade 1 © 2011 by Cheryl M. Sigmon, Scholastic Teaching Resources

- Reinforce the words in these lessons at every opportunity. Repetition throughout the year is what will cause the words to truly become "known words." Here are some ideas for achieving that:
  - Point out the words during reading lessons.
  - Encourage correct use of the words in students' writings.
  - Post the high-frequency words on a word wall in the classroom and the content words on cluster charts by subject.
  - Make other teachers aware of the words that you consider critical for students' growth.
  - With the occasional spare time that occurs in a classroom, review the week's words or review words from some of the previous weeks.

Above all else, have fun with this systematic plan for developing the vocabulary and word knowledge of your students!

Bibliography

The American Heritage dictionary of the English language. (2006). Boston: Houghton Mifflin Harcourt.

Bromley, K. (2007). Nine things every teacher should know about words and vocabulary instruction. *Journal of Adolescent & Adult Literacy, 50*(7), 528–537.

Fry, E., & Kress, J. (2006). *The reading teacher's book of lists* (5th ed.). San Francisco: Jossey-Bass.

Lehr, F., Osborne, J., & Hiebert, E. (2004). *A focus on vocabulary: Research-based practices in early reading*. Honolulu, HI: Pacific Resources for Education and Learning.

Mountain, L. (2005, May). ROOTing out meaning: More morphemic analysis for primary pupils. *The Reading Teacher, 58*(8), 742–749.

Pressley, M. (2002) *Comprehension instruction: What makes sense now? What might make sense soon? Reading online, International Reading Association*, December 2008, www.readingonline.org/articles/handbook/pressley/index.html.

Sigmon, C. (2007). *Just-right comprehension mini-lessons: Grade 1*. New York: Scholastic.

Torgesen, J. K., Rashotte, C. A., & Alexander, A. W. (2001). Principles of fluency instruction in reading: Relationships with established empirical outcomes. In M. Wolf (Ed.). *Dyslexia, fluency, and the brain*. (pp. 333–355) Austin, TX: Pro-Ed.

Zeno, S. M., Ivens, S. H., Millard, R. T., & Duvvuri, R. (1995). *The educator's word frequency guide*. Brewster, NY: Touchstone Applied Science Associates.

Recommended Web Sites

www.dictionary.com

www.rhymer.com

www.wordsmith.org

Day 1: Word Builder

Distribute the letter strip of the Lesson 1 Word Card and a small plastic bag to each student. Have students separate the letters. Review the letter names as you have students place them in alphabetical order: *a, e, m, n,* and *s.* You may want to write the letters on the board or place them in a pocket chart as you say their names.

Have students spell words as you call them out. Offer a sentence with each word to reinforce it and provide spelling support as necessary. Call out words in this order, arranged according to increasing difficulty:

a	am
an	same
man	name
me	names
men	

am

an

man

me

name

same

After students have time to spell each word, write the word on the board. Ask students to cross-check their spellings with yours and make corrections as necessary.

On the board or in a pocket chart, sort the written words according to spelling patterns:

-an	-am	-ame
an	am	name
man		same

After you've sorted the words, have students read over the words in each column, emphasizing the spelling pattern from the first vowel to the end of each word.

Then have students place the letters in a plastic bag and collect them.

Day 2: Dictation

Remind students that one of the biggest words from the previous day's lesson was the word *name.* Today they will use that word as they each build a sentence. Write the sentence frame on chart paper, repeating it so that each student can complete one frame. Try to line up each sentence so that students can easily see the predictable pattern. This week's sentence frame is:

My name is _____.

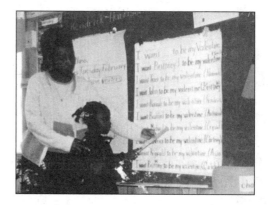

Read it aloud, and complete the first one with your name. Note that the first letter of a name is capitalized. Then invite each student to read the sentence and complete it by saying his or her name. Write the child's name in the blank, and continue until everyone has had a turn. Keep the chart handy; you'll need it for the lesson in Day 3.

Day 3: Sentence Builder

Choose 3 sentences from the chart created on Day 2 and write each on a separate sentence strip. Have the chart available for the lesson.

Begin by having each student come to the chart to read the sentence he or she dictated, pointing to each word as it is read. If students are having trouble with one-to-one correspondence (tapping a word as they say it), place your hand over theirs and guide the pointer.

When everyone has had a turn, take the first sentence strip you prepared, acknowledge whose sentence it is, and read the sentence aloud, pointing to each word as you go. Then take your scissors and cut the sentence apart, word by word, so students see that sentences are made up of individual words. Pass out the words to several students, giving the name to the student who dictated that sentence. Ask these students to come to the front of the class and arrange themselves in the order of the sentence, from left to right, offering assistance as necessary. Walk behind the students as they hold up their word card, and ask the class to read the sentence aloud together.

Repeat this procedure with the two remaining sentence strips you have prepared.

Day 4: Rhymer

Distribute the plastic bags containing the letters from Day 1. Tell students that some special words can help them spell many other words. Ask them to find the letters *m, a,* and *n* in their bags and then place them on their desk in order. Write the letters on the board; then look at the word and say *man,* running your finger under the letters as you do. Now remove the letter *m* from the word, and ask students:

If we wanted to write the word can, *what letter would we use instead of the* m?

Guide students to say *c.* Write a *c* on the board and read the word aloud, asking students to join in.

Continue to ask what change needs to be made as you progress through

fan

pan

tan

Dan*

ran

van

* Point out that names always begin with a capital letter.

Keep a running list of the words you make, and pause to discuss the meaning of each, providing a quick definition and sample sentence as needed.

If time allows, let students choose one of the words to illustrate. Invite them to write the word underneath if they are at the developmental stage to do so.

Day 5: Word Smart

Distribute the Lesson 1 Word Card, prepared as described on page 14. Have students break apart the words and arrange them across the top of their desks, leaving work space below. (Since this is the first time students are doing this, you may need to model how to tear apart the words and arrange them.)

Write the words on the board and read through them, having students point to the corresponding word on their desks.

Ask students to respond to your questions by picking up the correct word(s) and holding it so that you can see their answers. If there are more than 2 correct words, ask them to show only 2— one in each hand. Ask students the following questions, stopping if students lose attention or get frustrated.

Can you find . . .

- a word that has 2 letters?

- a word that has 3 letters?

- a word that has 4 letters?

- a word that starts with the letter *m*?

- a word that ends with the letter *m*?

- a word that rhymes with *pan*?

- a word that rhymes with *frame*?

- a word that rhymes with *tree*?

- two words that rhyme with each other?

- a word that means the opposite of *different*?

- a word that fits in this sentence: "When your _____ is called, get in line"?

- a word that fits in this sentence: "Will you go to the office with _____?"

Ask students to gather their word cards and place them in a plastic bag with the letters from this week's Word Card.

✳ Homework ✳

Send the letters and words home with each student. Parents can use the words as flash cards and the letters to practice making words, as described in the Parent-Child Word Work sheet.

Day 1: Word Builder

Distribute the letter strip of the Lesson 2 Word Card and a small plastic bag to each student. Have students separate the letters. Review the letter names as you have students place them in alphabetical order: *a, g, i, k, l, n, w.* You may want to write the letters on the board or place them in a pocket chart as you say their names.

Have students spell words as you call them out. Offer a sentence with each word to reinforce it and provide spelling support as necessary. Call out words in this order, arranged according to increasing difficulty:

in	wink
win	wing
kin	king
ink	walk
link	walking

in

win

wing

king

walk

walking

After students have time to spell each word, write the word on the board. Ask students to cross-check their spellings with yours and make corrections as necessary.

On the board or in a pocket chart, sort the written words according to spelling patterns:

-in	-ink	-ing
win	link	wing
kin	wink	walking
		king

After you've sorted the words, have students read over the words you've written in each column, emphasizing the spelling pattern from the first vowel to the end of each word.

Then have students place the letters in a plastic bag and collect them.

Day 2: Dictation

Remind students that the biggest word from the previous day's lesson was *walking.* Today they will use that word as they each build a sentence. Write the sentence frame on chart paper, repeating it so that each student can complete one frame. Try to line up each sentence so that students can easily see the predictable pattern. This week's sentence frame is

I am walking to the _____.

Read it aloud, and complete the first one with your own word. Then invite each student to read the sentence and complete it by saying where they are walking. Write the destination in the blank, and continue until everyone has had a turn. You may want to write each student's name on the chart after the sentence he or she dictates, to increase the sense of ownership of the activity. Keep the chart handy; you'll need it for the lesson in Day 3.

Day 3: Sentence Builder

Choose 3 sentences from the chart created on Day 2 and write each on a separate sentence strip. Have the chart available for the lesson.

Begin by having each student come to the chart to read the sentence he or she dictated, pointing to each word as it is read. If students are having trouble with one-to-one correspondence (tapping a word as they say it), place your hand over theirs and guide the pointer.

When everyone has had a turn, take the first sentence strip you prepared, acknowledge whose sentence it is, and read the sentence aloud, pointing to each word as you go. Then take your scissors and cut the sentence apart, word by word, so students see that sentences are made up of individual words. Pass out the words to several students, giving the location to the student who dictated that sentence. Ask these students to come to the front of the class and arrange themselves in the order of the sentence, from left to right, offering assistance as necessary. Walk behind the students as they hold up their word card, and ask the class to read the sentence aloud together.

Repeat this procedure with the two remaining sentence strips you have prepared.

Day 4: Rhymer

Distribute the plastic bags containing the letters from Day 1. Tell students that some special words can help them spell many other words. Ask them to find the letters *w, i, n* in their bags and then place them on their desk in order. Write the letters on the board; then look at the word and say *win*, running your finger under the letters as you do. Now remove the letter *w* from the word, and ask students:

If we wanted to write the word bin*, what letter would we use instead of* w?

Guide students to say *b*. Write a *b* on the board and read the word aloud, asking students to join in.

Continue to ask what change needs to be made as you progress through

din

fin

kin

pin

tin

Keep a running list of the words you make, and pause to discuss the meaning of each, providing a quick definition and sample sentence as needed.

If time allows, let students choose one of the words to illustrate. Invite them to write the word underneath if they are at the developmental stage to do so.

Day 5: Word Smart

Distribute the Lesson 2 Word Card, prepared as described on page 14. Have students break apart the words and arrange them across the top of their desks, leaving work space below. Write the words on the board and read through them, having students point to the corresponding word on their desks.

Ask students to respond to your questions by picking up the correct word(s) and holding it so that you can see their answers. If there are more than 2 correct words, ask them to show only 2— one in each hand. Ask students the following questions, stopping if students lose attention or get frustrated.

Can you find . . .

- a word with 2 letters?
- a word with 3 letters?
- a word with 4 letters?
- the word that has the most letters?
- a word that starts with the /w/ sound?
- a word that starts with the /k/ sound?
- a word that ends with the /n/ sound?
- a word that ends with the *-ing* pattern?
- a word that is the ruler in some countries but not in the United States?
- a word that has 2 syllables or beats?
- a word that rhymes with *pin*?
- a word that rhymes with *sing*?
- a word that has the little word *in* hiding inside?

Ask students to gather their word cards and place them in a plastic bag with the letters from this week's Word Card.

✳ Homework ✳

Send the letters and words home with each student. Parents can use the words as flash cards and the letters to practice making words, as described in the Parent-Child Word Work sheet.

Day 1: Word Builder

Distribute the letter strip of the Lesson 3 Word Card and a small plastic bag to each student. Have students separate the letters. Review the letter names as you have students place them in alphabetical order: *a, e, l, l, m, s, s, t*. You may want to write the letters on the board or place them in a pocket chart as you say their names.

Have students spell words as you call them out. Offer a sentence with each word to reinforce it and provide spelling support as necessary. Call out words in this order, arranged according to increasing difficulty:

at	all
mat	mall
sat	tall
set	small
let	smallest
met	

at

sat

let

met

tall

small

After students have time to spell each word, write the word on the board. Ask students to cross-check their spellings with yours and make corrections as necessary.

On the board or in a pocket chart, sort the written words according to spelling patterns:

-at	-et	-all
at	set	all
mat	let	mall
sat	met	tall
		small

After you've sorted the words, have students read over the words you've written in each column, emphasizing the spelling pattern from the first vowel to the end of each word.

Then have students place the letters in a plastic bag and collect them.

Day 2: Dictation

Remind students that one of the biggest words from the previous day's lesson was *small*. Today they will use that word as they each build a sentence. Write the sentence frame on chart paper, repeating it so that each student can complete one frame. Try to line up each sentence so that students can easily see the predictable pattern. This week's sentence frame is

A _____ is a small pet.

Read it aloud, and complete the first one with your choice of pet. Then invite each student to read the sentence and complete it with a type of pet. Write the contribution in the blank, and continue until everyone has had a turn. You may want to write each student's name next to the sentence he or she dictates, to increase the sense of ownership of the activity. Keep the chart handy; you'll need it for the lesson in Day 3.

Day 3: Sentence Builder

Choose 3 sentences from the chart created on Day 2 and write each on a separate sentence strip. Have the chart available for the lesson.

Begin by having each student come to the chart to read the sentence he or she dictated, pointing to each word as it is read. If students are having trouble with one-to-one correspondence (tapping a word as they say it), place your hand over theirs and guide the pointer.

When everyone has had a turn, take the first sentence strip you prepared, acknowledge whose sentence it is, and read the sentence aloud, pointing to each word as you go. Then take your scissors and cut the sentence apart, word by word, so students see that sentences are made up of individual words. Pass out the words to several students, giving the name of the pet to the student who dictated that sentence. Ask these students to come to the front of the class and arrange themselves in the order of the sentence, from left to right, offering assistance as necessary. Walk behind the students as they hold up their word card, and ask the class to read the sentence aloud together.

Repeat this procedure with the two remaining sentence strips you have prepared.

Day 4: Rhymer

Distribute the plastic bags containing the letters from Day 1. Tell students that some special words can help them spell many other words. Ask them to find the letters *m, a, t* in their bags and then place them on their desk in order. Write the letters on the board; then look at the word and say *mat*, running your finger under the letters as you do. Now remove the letter *m* from the word, and ask students:

If we wanted to write the word sat, *what letter would we use instead of the* m?

Guide students to say *s*. Write an *s* on the board and read the word aloud, asking students to join in.

Continue to ask what change needs to be made as you progress through

bat

cat

fat

hat

pat

rat

vat

Keep a running list of the words you make, and pause to discuss the meaning of each, providing a quick definition and sample sentence as needed.

If time allows, let students choose one of the words to illustrate. Invite them to write the word underneath if they are at the developmental stage to do so.

Day 5: Word Smart

Distribute the Lesson 3 Word Card, prepared as described on page 14. Have students tear the words apart and arrange them across the top of their desks, leaving work space below. Write the words on the board and read through them, having students point to the corresponding word on their desks.

Ask students to respond to your questions by picking up the correct word(s) and holding it so that you can see their answers. If there are more than 2 correct words, ask them to show only 2— one in each hand. Ask students the following questions, stopping if students lose attention or get frustrated.

Can you find . . .

- a word with 2 letters?
- a word with 3 letters?
- a word with 4 letters?
- a word with 5 letters?
- a word that starts with the /t/ sound?
- a word that ends with the /t/ sound?
- a word that ends with the -*all* pattern?
- a word that rhymes with *cat*?
- a word that rhymes with *vet*?
- two words that rhyme with each other?
- a word with 3 tall letters?

Ask students to gather their word cards and place them in a plastic bag with the letters from this week's Word Card.

✳ Homework ✳

Send the letters and words home with each student. Parents can use the words as flash cards and the letters to practice making words, as described in the Parent-Child Word Work sheet.

Day 1: Word Builder

Distribute the letter strip of the Lesson 4 Word Card and a small plastic bag to each student. Have students separate the letters. Review the letter names as you have students place them in alphabetical order: *a, i, n, p, t.* You may want to write the letters on the board or place them in a pocket chart as you say their names.

Have students spell words as you call them out. Offer a sentence with each word to reinforce it and provide spelling support as necessary. Call out words in this order, arranged according to increasing difficulty:

in	tan
tin	pan
pin	pain
nap	paint
tap	

in

pin

tap

tan

pan

paint

After students have time to spell each word, write the word on the board. Ask students to cross-check their spellings with yours to spell correctly. Sort your written word list according to any spelling patterns, such as:

-in	-ap	-an
in	nap	an
tin	tap	tan
pin		pan

After you've sorted the words, have students read over the words you've written in each column, emphasizing the spelling pattern from the first vowel to the end of each word.

Then have students place the letters in a plastic bag and collect them.

Day 2: Dictation

Remind students that the biggest word from the previous day's lesson was *paint*. Today they will use that word as they each build a sentence. Write the sentence frame on chart paper, repeating it so that each student can complete one frame. Try to line up each sentence so that students can easily see the predictable pattern. This week's sentence frame is

I will paint a _____.

Read it aloud, and complete the first one with an item you would like to paint. Then invite each student to read the sentence and complete it by saying what he or she would like to paint. Write the item in the blank, and continue until everyone has had a turn. You may want to write each student's name next to the sentence he or she dictates, to increase the sense of ownership of the activity. Keep the chart handy; you'll need it for the lesson in Day 3.

Day 3: Sentence Builder

Choose 3 sentences from the chart created on Day 2 and write each on a separate sentence strip. Have the chart available for the lesson.

Begin by having each student come to the chart to read the sentence he or she dictated, pointing to each word as it is read. If students are having trouble with one-to-one correspondence (tapping a word as they say it), place your hand over theirs and guide the pointer.

When everyone has had a turn, take the first sentence strip you prepared, acknowledge whose sentence it is, and read the sentence aloud, pointing to each word as you go. Then take your scissors and cut the sentence apart, word by word, so students see that sentences are made up of individual words. Pass out the words to several students, giving the name of the item to the student who dictated that sentence. Ask these students to come to the front of the class and arrange themselves in the order of the sentence, from left to right, offering assistance as necessary. Walk behind the students as they hold up their word card, and ask the class to read the sentence aloud together.

Repeat this procedure with the two remaining sentence strips you have prepared.

Day 4: Rhymer

Distribute the plastic bags containing the letters from Day 1. Tell students that some special words can help them spell many other words. Ask them to find the letters *t, a, p* in their bags and then place them on their desk in order. Write the letters on the board; then look at the word and say *tap*, running your finger under the letters as you do. Now remove the letter *t* from the word, and ask students:

If we wanted to write the word nap, *what letter would we use add in front of the* ap *that would make the /n/ sound?*

Guide students to say *n*. Write an *n* on the board and read the word aloud, asking students to join in.

Continue to ask what change needs to be made as you progress through

cap

gap

lap

map

rap

sap

zap

Keep a running list of the words you make, and pause to discuss the meaning of each, providing a quick definition and sample sentence as needed.

If time allows, let students choose one of the words to illustrate. Invite them to write the word underneath if they are at the developmental stage to do so.

Day 5: Word Smart

Distribute the Lesson 4 Word Card, prepared as described on page 14. Have students break apart the words and arrange them across the top of their desks, leaving work space below. Write the words on the board and read through them, having students point to the corresponding word on their desks.

Ask students to respond to your questions by picking up the correct word(s) and holding it so that you can see their answers. If there are more than 2 correct words, ask them to show only 2—one in each hand. Ask students the following questions, stopping if students lose attention or get frustrated.

Can you find . . .

- a word with 2 letters?
- a word with 5 letters?
- a word that starts with a /p/ sound?
- a word that has the vowel *i* in it?
- a word that starts with the /t/ sound?
- a word that ends with the /t/ sound?
- a word that rhymes with *chin*?
- a word that fits in this sentence: "You can _____ your foot to the music"?
- a word with tall letters?
- a word that starts with a tall letter?
- a word that rhymes with *map*?
- a word that is the opposite of *out*?
- a word that is a synonym or means the same as *knock*?

Ask students to gather their word cards and place them in a plastic bag with the letters from this week's Word Card.

✳ Homework ✳

Send the letters and words home with each student. Parents can use the words as flash cards and the letters to practice making words, as described in the Parent-Child Word Work sheet.

Day 1: Word Builder

Distribute the letter strip of the Lesson 5 Word Card and a small plastic bag to each student. Have students separate the letters. Review the letter names as you have students place them in alphabetical order: *e, i, g, r, s,* and *t.* You may want to write the letters on the board or place them in a pocket chart as you say their names.

Have students spell words as you call them out. Offer a sentence with each word to reinforce it and provide spelling support as necessary. Call out words in this order, arranged according to increasing difficulty:

is	stir
it	rest
sit	tire
get	tiger
set	tigers
sir	

is
it
get
set
rest
tiger

After students have time to spell each word, write the word on the board. Ask students to cross-check their spellings with yours and make corrections as necessary.

On the board or in a pocket chart, sort the written words according to spelling patterns:

-et	-ir	-it
get	sir	sit
set	stir	

After you've sorted the words, have students read over the words you've written in each column, emphasizing the spelling pattern from the first vowel to the end of each word.

Then have students place the letters in a plastic bag and collect them.

Day 2: Dictation

Remind students that one of the biggest words from the previous day's lesson was *tiger.* Today they will use that word as they each build a sentence. Write the sentence frame on chart paper, repeating it so that each student can complete one frame. Try to line up each sentence so that students can easily see the predictable pattern. This week's sentence frame is

A tiger can _____ in the jungle.

Read it aloud, and complete the first one with a verb. Then invite each student to read the sentence and complete it with a verb. Write the verb in the blank, and continue until everyone has had a turn. You may want to write each student's name on the chart next to the sentence he or she dictates to increase ownership of the activity. Keep the chart handy; you'll need it for the lesson in Day 3.

Day 3: Sentence Builder

Choose 3 sentences from the chart created on Day 2 and write each on a separate sentence strip. Have the chart available for the lesson.

Begin by having each student come to the chart to read the sentence he or she dictated, pointing to each word as it is read. If students are having trouble with one-to-one correspondence (tapping a word as they say it), place your hand over theirs and guide the pointer.

When everyone has had a turn, take the first sentence strip you prepared, acknowledge whose sentence it is, and read the sentence aloud, pointing to each word as you go. Then take your scissors and cut the sentence apart, word by word, so students see that sentences are made up of individual words. Pass out the words to several students, giving the verb to the student who dictated that sentence. Ask these students to come to the front of the class and arrange themselves in the order of the sentence, from left to right, offering assistance as necessary. Walk behind the students as they hold up their word card, and ask the class to read the sentence aloud together.

Repeat this procedure with the two remaining sentence strips you have prepared.

Day 4: Rhymer

Distribute the plastic bags containing the letters from Day 1. Tell students that some special words can help them spell many other words. Ask them to find the letters *s, i, and t* in their bags and then place them on their desk in order. Write the letters on the board; then look at the word and say *sit*, running your finger under the letters as you do. Now remove the letter *s* from the word, and ask students:

If we wanted to write the word pit*, what letter would we use add in front of it that would make the /p/ sound?*

Guide students to say *p*. Write a *p* on the board and read the word aloud, asking students to join in.

Continue to ask what change needs to be made as you progress through

bit

fit

hit

kit

lit

wit

Keep a running list of the words you make, and pause to discuss the meaning of each, providing a quick definition and sample sentence as needed.

If time allows, let students choose one of the words to illustrate. Invite them to write the word underneath if they are at the developmental stage to do so.

Day 5: Word Smart

Distribute the Lesson 5 Word Card, prepared as described on page 14. Have students break apart the words and arrange them across the top of their desks, leaving work space below. Write the words on the board and read through them, having students point to the corresponding word on their desks.

Ask students to respond to your questions by picking up the correct word(s) and holding it so that you can see their answers. If there are more than 2 correct words, ask them to show only 2— one in each hand. Ask students the following questions, stopping if students lose attention or get frustrated.

Can you find . . .

- a word that has 2 letters?
- a word that has 3 letters?
- a word that has 4 letters?
- a word that has 5 letters?
- a word that starts with the /t/ sound?
- a word that ends with the /t/ sound?
- a word that starts with the /g/ sound?
- a word that has the /g/ sound in the middle?
- two words that have the same beginning sound?
- two words that rhyme with each other?
- a word that has a tall letter?
- a word that starts with the letter *s*?

Ask students to gather their word cards and place them in a plastic bag with the letters from this week's Word Card.

✳ Homework ✳

Send the letters and words home with each student. Parents can use the words as flash cards and the letters to practice making words, as described in the Parent-Child Word Work sheet.

Day 1: Meet the Words

Pass out the Lesson 6 Word Cards, prepared as described on pages 14–15. Have students break apart the 6 new words and spread them on their desks. Ask students to do the following:

- Hold up each card as you pronounce the word on it.
- Look at the word, read it aloud, and spell it with you.
- Return the word card to the top of their desk.

Then guide students through the following activities, keeping a quick but comfortable pace determined by students' engagement with the task. If students seem frustrated, slow down and model the action. Say to students:

| they |
| please |
| saw |
| pretty |
| went |
| want |

- Find the word *they* and put it in your work space.
- This word is used in place of the names of several people. I can say, "Emma and Tyesha are going to the circus." Or, I can say, "They are going to the circus."
- Point to the two letters at the beginning of the word that make the /th/ sound.
- Repeat after me these familiar words that start with the same sound: *this, those, the,* and *that.*
- Return the word *they* to the top of your desk. Find the word *please* and put it in your work space. This is a good-manners word that we use when we ask someone to do something for us.

- Put your finger under the 2 letters at the beginning that blend together to make the /pl/ sound.
- Repeat these words that have the same /pl/ sound at the beginning: *play, plow, plant,* and *place.*
- Put the word *please* back and get the word *saw.* This word is used in this sentence: *I saw you at the store yesterday.*
- Slide your finger underneath the letter that represents each sound as I say it. (/s/ /a/ /w/)
- Repeat these words that end with the same sound as *saw: flaw, slaw, jaw, raw,* and *paw.*
- Put *saw* with the other words and get the word *pretty.*
- Let's think of some words that mean the same as *pretty.* (*lovely, cute, beautiful, attractive, good-looking*)
- Listen to the syllables or beats in *pretty* as I clap them. (Say and clap the two syllables "pret-ty.") Now say and clap them with me. There are 2 syllables or beats in *pretty.*

- Put *pretty* back and find two words this time. Place *went* and *want* in your work space.
- Hold up the word *went.* This word fits in this sentence: *I went to the grocery store yesterday.*
- Hold up the word *want.* This word is used in this sentence: *I want you to go with me to the store.* It means I wish for you to go with me.
- These words look almost the same. Put your fingers on the letters that are different in these 2 words. (*e/a*) Put your finger on the letter in each word that makes the /w/ sound.
- Let's collect our new words and save them to use later in the week.

Distribute plastic bags and have students put the words in the bags. Collect them or have students store them in their desks.

Day 2: Word Whittle

Distribute the Lesson 6 words and have students place them across the top of their work space. Read through the clues one at a time. After the first clue is read, students select the words that fit and place them in their work space. For each subsequent clue in the set, they choose from their "whittled" selections, returning the ones that do not fit to the top of their work space. No new words can be added to the group after the first clue is given. After the final clue in a set, only one word will remain. Students return it to the top of their work space before the next set of clues is given.

First Word:
1. a word that has 4 letters (*they, went, want*)
2. a word that has the vowel *e* in it (*they, went*)
3. a word that has 2 tall letters in it (*they*)

Second Word:
1. a word that has the letter *t* in it (*they, went, want, pretty*)
2. a word that has the vowel *e* (*they, went, pretty*)
3. a word that rhymes with *sent* (*went*)

Third Word:
1. a word with the letter *w* in it (*went, want, saw*)
2. a word that ends with the /t/ sound (*went, want*)
3. a word that fits in this sentence: Do you _____to go with me to the movies? (*want*)

Fourth Word:
1. a word that has the vowel *e* in it (*please, pretty, went, they*)
2. a word that starts with the letter *p* (*please, pretty*)
3. a word that has two syllables or beats in it (*pretty*)

Have students return the words to the bags and store them for future use.

Day 3: Free Choice Activity Day

Choose one or two of these activities (see pages 18–20):

☐ Word Match   ☐ Word Pop   ☐ Word Swat

☐ Word Sort   ☐ Voice Choice   ☐ Cheer the Words

☐ Word Detective   ☐ Rhymer   ☐ Other: _____

Word Sort

If you choose Word Sort, here are categories that fit this week's words:

- words that start with the /w/ sound
- words with one syllable or beat
- words with some tall letters
- words with letters that drop below the line
- words that end in the /t/ sound

Day 4: Word Builder

Distribute the letter strip of the Lesson 6 Word Card to each student. Have students separate the letters, reviewing the letter names as you have students place them in alphabetical order: *e, n, p, s,* and *t.* You may want to write the letters on the board or place them in a pocket chart as you say their names.

Have students spell words as you call them out. Write each word on the board as students work, and offer a sentence to help them understand its meaning. Ask students to cross-check their spellings with yours and make corrections as necessary. Call out words in this increasingly difficult order.

set	ten	nest
pet	pen	sent
net	pest	spent

On the board or in a pocket chart, sort the written words according to spelling patterns, including -*est* and -*ent* if your students are ready:

-et	-en	-est	-ent
set	ten	pest	sent
pet	pen	nest	spent
net			

After you've sorted the words, have students read over the words you've written in each column, emphasizing the spelling pattern from the first vowel to the end of each word.

Focus on the -*et* words. Tell students that if they know this pattern, it can help them spell many other words. Invite students to brainstorm a list of other words that rhyme with *set*, recording them on the board: *bet, get, jet, let, met, vet, wet.*

You may repeat this process with the other spelling patterns as appropriate for your particular students.

When you've finished, have students place the letters in a plastic bag with this week's words and store them.

Day 5: Word Smart

Distribute the Lesson 6 words, and ask students to arrange them across the top of their desks, leaving work space below. Write the words on the board and read through them, having students point to the corresponding word on their desks.

Ask students to respond to your questions by picking up the correct word(s) and holding it so that you can see their answers. If there are more than 2 correct words, ask them to show only 2— one in each hand.

Can you find . . .

- a word that starts with the /s/ sound? the /w/ sound?
- a word that starts with the letter *p*?
- a word that ends with the /t/ sound?
- a word that has one syllable or beat? has 2 syllables or beats?
- a word that rhymes with *squeeze*? with *cent*?
- a word that means the same as *lovely*?
- a word that shows good manners?
- a word that has the little word *he* inside?
- two words you might use together when you ask for something you want very badly? (*pretty please*)

When you've finished, have students place the words in a plastic bag and store them.

❋ Homework ❋

Send the letters and words home with each student. Parents can use the words as flash cards and the letters to practice making words, as described in the Parent-Child Word Work sheet.

Day 1: Meet the Words

Pass out the Lesson 7 Word Cards, prepared as described on pages 14–15. Have students break apart the 6 new words and spread them on their desks. Ask students to do the following:

- Hold up each card as you pronounce the word on it.
- Look at the word, read it aloud, and spell it with you.
- Return the word card to the top of their desk.

Then guide students through the following activities, keeping a quick but comfortable pace determined by students' engagement with the task. If students seem frustrated, slow down and model the action. Say to students:

jump

who

help

after

well

our

- Put the word *jump* in your work space.
- This is a verb that shows action. Take your word *jump* and stand beside your desk and show me the action—let's jump!
- Now, sitting down again, put your finger under the letter that makes the /j/ sound. This is the same letter and sound in the words *jet, jelly,* and *jingle*.
- The letters *u-m-p* represent the sound /ump/. What words can we think of that rhyme with *jump*? (*bump, dump, hump, lump, pump, rump, stump*) We can spell all of those words because we know the *-ump* pattern!
- Put *jump* back and get the word *who*. The letters *w* and *h* in this word represent the /h/ sound. Most words that begin with *w* and *h* are pronounced /hw/ like in the words *what, when, where, whistle, wheel*. So *who* is different.

- *Who* relates to a person. Sometimes we use it to ask a question: Who is your brother? Or, we might say: I like students who study hard. Turn to your buddy and ask them a *who* question.
- Put *who* back and get the word *help*.
- Sometimes *help* is an action word. We might help a friend by picking up something dropped. Sometimes *help* means we're in trouble. If I scream "Help!" I need someone to come quickly!
- Share with a partner how you help your families at home. (After a minute, ask a few to share with the class.)
- Put *help* back and get the word *after*.
- This word has 2 syllables. Let's clap them together as we pronounce the syllables—*af* (clap) *-ter* (clap).

- *After* means following or behind. (Call 3 students to come to the front of the class. Line them up. Explain, "Mary comes first and Ethan comes *after* Mary. Then, Yvonne comes *after* Ethan." Ask some questions like, "Who comes before Ethan? Who comes after Mary?" Be sure they understand the concept of before and after.)
- Put *after* away and put *well* in your work space.
- Put your finger under the letter that makes the /w/ sound.
- The letters *e-l-l* represent the sound of the name of the letter *l*.
- Let's think of words that rhyme with *well*: *bell, dell, fell, gel, sell*.
- *Well* has a couple of very different meanings. Sometimes we use well to tell how we feel. I might say, "I don't feel well." Another meaning of *well* is a deep hole in the ground where water is stored. Some people get water in their homes from a well.
- Put *well* back and get the word *our*. This word tells that something belongs to several people, or to us—*our* books, *our* school, *our* families.
- This word also sounds just like another word spelled a little differently—*hour* (write this word). *Hour* relates to telling time. It's tricky that 2 words are pronounced the same but have different spellings and meanings! They're called homophones, and we'll see more of them in our reading and word study.
- Let's collect our new words and save them to use later in the week.

Distribute plastic bags and have students put the words in the bags. Collect them or have students store them in their desks.

Day 2: Word Whittle

Distribute the Lesson 7 words and have students place them across the top of their work space. Work through the following sets of clues as described on page 32.

First Word:
1. a word that has the vowel *e* in it (*help, well, after*)
2. a word that has the letter *l* in it (*help, well*)
3. a word that fits in this sentence: Can I _____ you get down from the tree? (*help*)

Second Word:
1. a word that has a tall letter in it (*help, who, well, after*)
2. a word that has 4 letters (*help, well*)
3. a word that starts the same way *wish* starts (*well*)

Third Word:
1. a word that has 4 letters (*help, jump, well*)
2. a word that ends with a /p/ sound (*help, jump*)
3. If you do what this word says, your feet will leave the floor! (*jump*)

Fourth Word:

1. a word that has the vowel *e* in it (*help, well, after*)
2. a word that has 2 tall letters in it (*help, well, after*)
3. a word that has 2 syllables (*after*)

Have students return the words to the plastic bags and store them for future use.

Day 3: Free Choice Activity Day

Choose one or two of these activities (see pages 18–20):

☐ Word Match ☐ Word Pop ☐ Word Swat
☐ Word Sort ☐ Voice Choice ☐ Cheer the Words
☐ Word Detective ☐ Rhymer ☐ Other: _____

Word Sort

If you choose Word Sort, here are categories that fit this week's words:

- words that end with the same sounds/letters
- words with 3, 4, or 5 letters
- words with 1 or 2 syllables
- words that start or end with a vowel/with a consonant

Day 4: Word Builder

Distribute the letter strip of the Lesson 7 Word Card to each student. Have students separate the letters, reviewing the letter names as you have students place them in alphabetical order: *a, e, f, n, n, o, o, r,* and *t.* You may want to write the letters on the board or place them in a pocket chart as you say their names.

Have students spell words as you call them out. Write each word on the board as students work and offer a sentence to help them understand its meaning. Ask students to cross-check their spellings with yours and make corrections as necessary. Call out words in this increasingly difficult order.

fan	rat	tear
tan	ear	after
ran	near	afternoon
fat	fear	

On the board or in a pocket chart, sort the written words according to the spelling patterns shown below. This week's words review the -*an* and -*at* patterns; you may include -*ear* if you're students are ready:

-an	-at	-ear
fan	fat	ear
tan	rat	near
ran		fear
		tear

After you've sorted the words, have students read over the words you've written in each column, emphasizing the spelling pattern from the first vowel to the end of each word.

Focus on the -*an* words. Tell students that if they know this pattern, it can help them spell many other words. Invite students to brainstorm a list of other words that rhyme with *fan,* recording them on the board: *Jan, ban, can, Dan, man, pan, Nan.*

Point out that names always begin with a capital letter. Repeat the process for the -*at* words, and with -*ear* if appropriate for your particular students.

When you've finished, have students place the letters in a plastic bag with this week's words and store them.

Day 5: Word Smart

Distribute the Lesson 7 words, and ask students to arrange them across the top of their desks, leaving work space below. Write the words on the board and read through them, having students point to the corresponding word on their desks.

Ask students to respond to your questions by picking up the correct word(s) and holding it so that you can see their answers. If there are more than 2 correct words, ask them to show only 2— one in each hand.

Can you find . . .

- a word that starts with the /h/ sound?
- a word that ends with the /p/ sound?
- a word that starts with the same sound as the word *walk*?
- a word that rhymes with *thump*?
- a word that rhymes with *bell*?
- a word that rhymes with *shoe*?
- a word that has 2 syllables?
- a word that has no tall letters or letters that go below the line?
- a word that fits in this sentence: "Can you _____ me find my classroom?"
- a word that either means "good" or "a deep hole that stores water?" that means the opposite of "before?"
- a word you might scream if you want someone to come quickly?

When you've finished, have students place the words in a plastic bag and store them.

✳ Homework ✳

Send the letters and words home with each student. Parents can use the words as flash cards and the letters to practice making words, as described in the Parent-Child Word Work sheet.

Day 1: Meet the Words

Pass out the Lesson 8 Word Cards, prepared as described on pages 14–15. Have students break apart the 6 new words and spread them on their desks. Ask students to do the following:

- Hold up each card as you pronounce the word on it.
- Look at the word, read it aloud, and spell it with you.
- Return the word card to the top of their desk.

Then guide students through the following activities, keeping a quick but comfortable pace determined by students' engagement with the task. If students seem frustrated, slow down and model the action. Say to students:

brown
not
what
get
good
there

- Find the word *brown* and put it in your workspace. Put your fingers under the first two letters that make the /br/ sound.

- Move your fingers to the next two letters that make the /ou/ sound we make when we are hurt. Now touch the last letter that makes the /n/ sound.

- The *–own* pattern helps us write words like *clown, town,* and *frown.*

- Pick up the word *brown* and find something in the room that is that color. (Have a few students share.)

- Return the word *brown* and put the word *not* in your workspace. Put your fingers under the first letter, *n*, which represents the /n/ sound.

- Now slide your fingers under the *o* and *t* and say /ot/. Then put /n/ and /ot/ together—*not!*

- We can spell many other words if we know the *-ot* pattern. Let's think of other words that rhyme with *not: cot, dot, got, hot, jot, lot, pot, rot, tot.*

- *Not* is a negative word, meaning "no." If you are not allowed to run in the classroom, that means no running is allowed.

- Return the word *not* and put the word *what* in your work space.

- Put your finger on the 2 letters that make the /hw/ sound. The letters *w* and *h* together usually represent the /hw/ sound.

- Put your finger on the letter that makes the /t/ sound at the end. Say the word with me: *what.*

- *What* is a question word. We use it in questions, such as "What time is it?" or "What is your name?"

- Return *what* and find the word *get.*

- Put your finger under the letter that represents each sound as I say it–/g/, /e/, /t/. Each letter represents one sound.

- What other word this week ends in the same sound, /t/? (*what*)

- Many words use the spelling pattern we see in *get.* If we know *get,* then we can read and write words like *pet, jet,* and *let.*

- Pull down the word *good* and place it next to *get.* What sound do these 2 words have in common? (/g/) That sound is represented by the letter *g;* point to it in both words.

- Put *get* with the other words and keep *good* in the work space.

- Put your finger under the letters that represent each sound as I say it: /g/ /oŏ/ /d/. Notice that the middle sound /oŏ/ is represented by two letters.

- What is a word that would mean the opposite of *good*?

- Can you cover 2 letters with your finger and make the word *go*?

- Return the word *good* and get the word *there.*

- Cover all letters except the first two with your fingers. *T* and *h* together represent the /th/ sound.

- *There* refers to place. *Step over there to wait.* I've never been *there!*

- Let's collect our new words and save them to use later in the week.

Distribute plastic bags and have students put the words in the bags. Collect them or have students store them in their desks.

Day 2: Word Whittle

Distribute the Lesson 8 words and have students place them across the top of their work space. Work through the following sets of clues as described on page 32.

First Word:
1. a word that has more than 3 letters in it (*brown, what, good, there*)
2. a word that has 2 tall letters in it (*there, what*)
3. a word that ends with the vowel *e* (*there*)

Second Word:
1. a word with the vowel *o* in it (*brown, not, good*)
2. a word with an *n* in it (*brown, not*)
3. a word that is a color (*brown*)

Third Word:
1. a word that ends with a tall letter (*what, good, get*)
2. a word that starts with the /g/ sound (*good, get*)
3. a word that has 2 of the same letter (*good*)

Fourth Word:

1. a word that ends with a *t* (*what, not, get*)
2. a word with 3 letters (*not, get*)
3. a word that starts with the /g/ sound (*get*)

Have students return the word cards to the plastic bags and store them for future use.

Day 3: Free Choice Activity Day

Choose one or two of these activities (see pages 18–20):

☐ Word Match ☐ Word Pop ☐ Word Swat

☐ Word Sort ☐ Voice Choice ☐ Cheer the Words

☐ Word Detective ☐ Rhymer ☐ Other: _____

Word Sort

If you choose Word Sort, here are categories that fit this week's words:

- words with letters that start with blended sounds
- words with the *-at* spelling pattern
- words with letters that go above/below the line
- words that start with the /g/ sound
- words that end with the /t/ sound

Day 4: Word Builder

Distribute the letter strip of the Lesson 8 Word Card to each student. Have students separate the letters, reviewing the letter names as you have students place them in alphabetical order: *d, e, o, p, s, t,* and *t.* You may want to write the letters on the board or place them in a pocket chart as you say their names.

Have students spell words as you call them out. Write each word on the board as students work and offer a sentence to help them understand its meaning. Ask students to cross-check their spellings with yours and make corrections as necessary. Call out words in this increasingly difficult order.

top	dot	spot
sop	tot	spotted
stop	pot	

On the board or in a pocket chart, sort the written words according to the spelling patterns below.

-op	-ot
top	dot
sop	tot
stop	pot
	spot

After you've sorted the words, have students read over the words you've written in each column, emphasizing the spelling pattern from the first vowel to the end of each word.

Focus on the *-op* words. Tell students that if they know this pattern, it can help them spell many other words. Invite students to brainstorm a list of other words that rhyme with *top*, recording them on the board (include words with blends if your students are ready): *bop, cop, hop, mop, pop, clop, drop.*

You may repeat this process with the other spelling pattern as appropriate for your particular students.

When you've finished, have students place the letters in a plastic bag with this week's words and store them.

Day 5: Word Smart

Distribute the Lesson 8 words, and ask students to arrange them across the top of their desks, leaving work space below. Write the words on the board and read through them, having students point to the corresponding word on their desks.

Ask students to respond to your questions by picking up the correct word(s) and holding it so that you can see their answers. If there are more than 2 correct words, ask them to show only 2— one in each hand.

Can you find . . .

- a word that starts with the /g/ sound?
- a word that ends with the /t/ sound?
- a word that has one syllable or beat?
- a word that rhymes with *hood*?
- a word that rhymes with *jet*?
- a word that rhymes with *clown*?
- a word that has the word *at* hiding inside of it?
- a word that describes the kind of student we would all like to be?
- a word that has the word *here* inside?
- a word that fits in this sentence: "_____ time is it?"
- a word that has two of the same letters in it?

✳ Homework ✳

Send the letters and words home with each student. Parents can use the words as flash cards and the letters to practice making words, as described in the Parent-Child Word Work sheet.

Day 1: Meet the Words

Pass out the Lesson 9 Word Cards, prepared as described on pages 14–15. Have students break apart the 6 new words and spread them on their desks. Ask students to do the following:

- Hold up each card as you pronounce the word on it.
- Look at the word, read it aloud, and spell it with you.
- Return the word card to the top of their desk.

Then guide students through the following activities, keeping a quick but comfortable pace determined by students' engagement with the task. If students seem frustrated, slow down and model the action. Say to students:

thank

some

stop

had

his

her

- Find the word *thank* and put it in your work space. *Thank you* is a polite term we use to tell someone we appreciate what they've done for us.
- Count the letters that are tall and go above the line.
- Trace around the outline of the word with your finger.
- Put *thank* away and get the word *some*.
- *Some* is used 3 times in this sentence: *Flowers need some water, some soil, and some sunlight to grow.* It means a bit—not too much, not too little.
- Put your finger on the letter that represents this sound: /s/. What letter in the word represents the /m/ sound? Point to the *m* and say /m/, *some*.
- Return *some* and get the word *stop*.
- Put your finger under the 2 letters that make the sounds /st/. The sounds of the letters *s* and *t* blend together to make the /st/ sound. But you can hear /s/ and /t/ in the sound; they go together. Let's say it together: /st/, *stop*.
- Put your finger under the letter that represents the last sound in *stop*, /p/. (Write the word *stop* on the board and draw an octagon around it.) Where would you see such a sign? What must drivers do when they see this sign?
- Return this word and find all of the words beginning with the letter *h*; put them in your work space. There are three words that start with *h*: *had, his,* and *her*.
- Each of these words has a vowel in the middle. Point to the vowels in each word: *a* in *had, i* in *his,* and *e* in *her*.

- Point to the word that ends with a /d/ sound. Then the /s/ sound, and last, the /r/ sound.
- Find *had*. This word is used in this sentence: *We had hamburgers for lunch. Had* is a verb in a sentence that tells us something has happened in the past.
- Find the word *his*. This word is used to tell that something belongs to a male, such as *His books fell out of his desk.*
- Find the word *her*. This word is sometimes used to tell that something belongs to a female, such as *Her books fell out of her desk.* So, *his* refers to males—boys, men, or even male animals, and *her* refers to females—girls, women, and even female animals: *The duckling waddled behind her mother.*
- Let's collect our new words and save them to use later in the week.

Day 2: Word Whittle

Distribute the Lesson 9 words and have students place them across the top of their work space. Work through the following sets of clues as described on page 32.

First Word:
1. a word that starts with the /h/ sound (*had, his, her*)
2. a word that shows that something belongs to someone (*his, her*)
3. a word that can show something belongs to a female—a girl, woman or female animal (*her*)

Second Word:
1. a word whose first letter goes above the line (*had, his, her*)
2. a word that means something belongs to a boy or a girl (*his, her*)
3. a word that ends with the letter *s* (*his*)

Third Word:
1. a word that has more than 3 letters (*some, thank, stop*)
2. a word that starts with the letter *s* (*some, stop*)
3. a word that you would find on a sign on a street corner (*stop*)

Fourth Word:
1. a word that has at least one tall letter above the line (*had, his, her, thank, stop*)
2. a word that has four or more letters (*thank, stop*)
3. a word that rhymes with *tank* (*thank*)

Have students return the words to the plastic bags and store them for future use.

Day 3: Free Choice Activity Day

Choose one or two of these activities (see pages 18–20):

- ☐ Word Match
- ☐ Word Pop
- ☐ Word Swat
- ☐ Word Sort
- ☐ Voice Choice
- ☐ Cheer the Words
- ☐ Word Detective
- ☐ Rhymer
- ☐ Other: _____

Word Sort

If you choose Word Sort, here are categories that fit this week's words:

- words that start with /h/ sound
- words that show that something belongs to someone
- words with 3, 4, or 5 letters

Day 4: Word Builder

Distribute the letter strip of the Lesson 9 Word Card to each student. Have students separate the letters, reviewing the letter names as you have students place them in alphabetical order: *a, f, h, k, l, n, t,* and *u.* You may want to write the letters on the board or place them in a pocket chart as you say their names.

Have students spell words as you call them out. Write each word on the board as students work, and offer a sentence to help them understand its meaning. Ask students to cross-check their spellings with yours and make corrections as necessary. Call out words in this increasingly difficult order, including the shaded word if your students are ready:

at	hut	tank
hat	hunt	thank
fat	hunk	thankful
flat	Hank*	

* Point out that names always begin with a capital letter.

On the board or in a pocket chart, sort the written words according to the spelling patterns:

-at	-ank
at	Hank
hat	thank
fat	
flat	

After you've sorted the words, have students read over the words you've written in each column, emphasizing the spelling pattern from the vowel to the end of each word.

Focus on the *-ank* words. Tell students that if they know this pattern, it can help them spell many other words. Invite students to brainstorm a list of other words that rhyme with *tank,* recording them on the board: *bank, dank, Frank, prank, rank, sank, thank.*

You may repeat this process with the other spelling patterns, as appropriate for your particular students.

When you've finished, have students place the letters in a plastic bag with this week's words and store them.

Day 5: Word Smart

Distribute the Lesson 9 words, and ask students to arrange them across the top of their desks, leaving work space below. Write the words on the board and read through them, having students point to the corresponding word on their desks.

Ask students to respond to your questions by picking up the correct word(s) and holding it so that you can see their answers. If there are more than 2 correct words, ask them to show only 2— one in each hand. *Can you find . . .*

- a word that rhymes with *mad*?
- a word that rhymes with *mop*?
- a word that is often seen on a sign?
- a word that starts with the /h/ sound?
- a word that starts with the /th/ sound?
- a word that has only 1 tall letter above the line?
- a word that has no tall letters?
- a word that is polite?
- a word that ends with the /d/ sound?
- a word that ends with the /p/ sound?
- a word that fits in this sentence: "Maria is taking ___ brother to the movies"?
- a word that starts with the same sound as the word *summer*?

When you've finished, have students place the words in a plastic bag and store them.

❊ Homework ❊

Send the letters and words home with each student. Parents can use the words as flash cards and the letters to practice making words, as described in the Parent-Child Word Work sheet.

Day 1: Meet the Words

Pass out the Lesson 10 Word Cards, prepared as described on pages 14–15. Have students break apart the 6 new words and spread them on their desks. Ask students to do the following:

- Hold up each card as you pronounce the word on it.
- Look at the word, read it aloud, and spell it with you.
- Return the word card to the top of their desk.

Then guide students through the following activities, keeping a quick but comfortable pace determined by students' engagement with the task. If students seem frustrated, slow down and model the action. Say to students:

under

black

white

must

say

soon

- Find the word *under* and put it in your work space. *Under* means "beneath or below." Take the word *under* and hold it *under* your desk. Now hold it *under* your chin.

- Cover the last 3 letters with your finger. The letters *u* and *n* are left; let's blend them together: /u/, /n/, /un/. This letter combination is one we will see often.

- Let's clap the beats to this word as we say it together: /un/, /der/. It has two beats. Let's do that again: /un/, /der/, *under*!

- Put *under* away and put *black* in your work space. Put your finger under the first two letters and listen to me blend those sounds together: /bl/. Let's make the sound together: /bl/.

- Cover the *b* and *l* with your finger and look at the last 3 letters. They represent the sound /ack/. That's an important spelling pattern for us to know. If we know *-ack*, we can write words like *tack, sack, Jack, slack, rack,* and even the word *quack*.

- Black is the darkest shade on the color scale. Find the word *white* and put it beside *black*. Now we have the lightest and darkest colors in the whole range of colors.

- Put *black* back with the other words. Cover the last 3 letters of *white* with your hand. What's left is *w* and *h*. Together they make the /hw/ sound in this word. It's the same sound that starts the words *what, when, why,* and *whale*. Let's all make the /hw/ sound.

- Let's clap the beats to this word as we say it together: *white*. There's only one beat. Let's do that again: *white*.

- Put *white* back and get the word *must*.

- This word tells something that has to be done as in this sentence: *We must put on our coats to go outside.*

- Put your finger on the letter that represents the beginning /m/ sound. Yes, *m* represents the /m/ sound.

- Let's clap the beats to this word as we say it together: *must*. There's only one beat. Now we *must* put the word *must* with the other words on our desk.

- Find the words *say* and *soon* and put them in your work space.

- Put your fingers on the letter in each word that represents the /s/ sound. *S* represents the /s/ sound.

- Cover the letter *s* in the word *say*. Now let's say *say* without the /s/ sound at the beginning: /ā/. The letters *a* and *y* together represent the sound /ā/, which we call the long-*a* sound. The *ay* spelling pattern can help us spell many words. Let's see how many words we can come up with that rhyme with *say: bay, cay, day, hay, Jay, lay, may, pay, ray, way.* (Write words on the board as students suggest them.)

- Now, can you say *soon*? Notice how the two *o*'s look like eyes in the middle of this word. *Soon* means quickly or shortly.

- Put your finger on the letter that makes the /n/ sound.

- Soon we will know all of these helpful words! That means we'll know them very quickly after we study them this week!

- Let's collect our new words and save them to use later in the week.

Day 2: Word Whittle

Distribute the Lesson 10 words and have students place them across the top of their work space. Work through the following sets of clues as described on page 32.

First Word:

1. a word that has fewer than 5 letters (*must, say, soon*)
2. a word that starts with the /s/ sound (*say, soon*)
3. a word that rhymes with May (*say*)

Second Word:

1. a word that has 5 letters (*black, white, under*)
2. a word that is a color (*black, white*)
3. a word that rhymes with *kite* (*white*)

Third Word:

1. a word that has 2 vowels (*white, soon, under*)
2. a word that has a tall letter above the line (*white, under*)
3. a word that has 2 syllables or beats (*under*)

Fourth Word:

1. a word that has the letter *s* in it (*must, say, soon*)
2. a word that has 4 letters in it (*must, soon*)
3. a word that fits in this sentence: We will _____ know all of these words. (*soon*)

Day 3: Free Choice Activity Day

Choose one or two of these activities (see pages 18–20):

☐ Word Match ☐ Word Pop ☐ Word Swat

☐ Word Sort ☐ Voice Choice ☐ Cheer the Words

☐ Word Detective ☐ Rhymer ☐ Other: _____

Word Sort

If you choose Word Sort, here are categories that fit this week's words:

- words with letters that start with blended sounds (or partner letters).

- words that start with the /s/ sound

- words that are colors

- words with 3, 4, or 5 letters

- words with long vowel sounds

- words that end with the /t/ sound

Day 4: Word Builder

Distribute the letter strip of the Lesson 10 Word Card to each student. Have students separate the letters, reviewing the letter names as you have students place them in alphabetical order: *d, e, h, n, r, t,* and *u.* You may want to write the letters on the board or place them in a pocket chart as you say their names.

Have students spell words as you call them out. Write each word on the board as students work, and offer a sentence to help them understand its meaning. Ask students to cross-check their spellings with yours and make corrections as necessary. Call out words in this increasingly difficult order, including the shaded words if your students are ready:

den	then	*hunt*
hen	run	*hunted*
ten	*runt*	*thunder*

On the board or in a pocket chart, sort the written words according to the *-en* spelling pattern, including *-unt* if desired.

-en	-unt
hen	*runt*
ten	*hunt*
den	
then	

After you've sorted the words, have students read over the words you've written in each column, emphasizing the spelling pattern from the first vowel to the end of each word.

Focus on the *-en* words. Tell students that if they know this pattern, it can help them spell many other words. Invite students to brainstorm a list of other words that rhyme with *hen*, recording them on the board: *Ben, den, men, pen, ten, yen, wren.*

You may repeat this process with the other spelling pattern as appropriate for your particular students.

Day 5: Word Smart

Distribute the Lesson 10 words, and ask students to arrange them across the top of their desks, leaving work space below. Write the words on the board and read through them, having students point to the corresponding word on their desks.

Ask students to respond to your questions by picking up the correct word(s) and holding it so that you can see their answers. *Can you find . . .*

- a word that rhymes with *bright*? with *Jack*?
- a word that rhymes with *rust*? with *moon*?
- a word that means "quickly?"
- a word that means "to speak?"
- a word that starts with the /bl/ sound?
- a word that starts with the /s/ sound?
- a word that ends with the /t/ sound?
- a word that starts with the /hw/ sound?
- a word that names a color?
- a word that means opposite of *over*?
- a word that fits in this sentence: "We need to ____ 'please' and 'thank you' to be polite"?
- a word that has 2 syllables or beats?

✳ Homework ✳

Send the letters and words home with each student. Parents can use the words as flash cards and the letters to practice making words, as described in the Parent-Child Word Work sheet.

Day 1: Meet the Words

Pass out the Lesson 11 Word Cards, prepared as described on pages 14–15. Have students break apart the 6 new words and spread them on their desks. Ask students to do the following:

- Hold up each card as you pronounce the word on it.
- Look at the word, read it aloud, and spell it with you.
- Return the word card to the top of their desk.

Then guide students through the following activities, saying:

- Put the word *down* in your work space.
- Put your finger on the letter that represents the /d/ sound. *D* represents the /d/ sound.

down

where

funny

that

out

into

- Put your finger on the letter that represents the /n/ sound at the end. *N* represents the /n/ sound. This word rhymes with *clown*, *frown*, and *drown*.
- *Down* means the opposite of *up*. Hold this word up. Now bring it back down to your desk and place it with the other words.
- Where is the word *where*? Find it and put it in your work space.
- *Where* is a word that tells about location. *Where* is your desk? *Where* do you live?
- Put your finger on the 2 beginning letters that together represent the /hw/ sound, *w* and *h*. We studied the word *white* last week; it begins with the same sound: /hw/, *white*; /hw/, *where*.

- How many tall letters does this word have? Trace the word with your fingers and notice how it goes up over the tall *h*.
- Put *where* back and get the word *funny*.
- Things that are funny might be jokes, riddles, some movies, and cartoons. Funny things make us laugh.
- Put your finger over the last 2 letters. Now you have the word *fun*.
- When we add the *n-y* back, we have *funny*. There are 2 of the same consonant together in this word. What is it?
- Put *funny* back and put *that* in your work space. *That* is a word that tells us which one—*that* student, *that* pencil.
- Put your finger under the two letters that work together to make the /th/ sound. This is the same sound in the words *they* and *there*, which we've already studied.

- Put your finger under the letter that represents the /t/ sound at the end. There are 2 words hiding in this word. Cover the first letter with your finger, and you'll find *hat*. Cover the first 2 letters and you'll find *at*.
- Put *that* back and put *out* in your work space.
- What word means the opposite of *out*? (*in*)
- Point to the letter that represents the /t/ sound at the end.
- The words *shout* and *pout* rhyme with *out*. *Out* can help us spell those words. What letter can we put in front of *out* to make *pout*? What 2 letters that represent the /sh/ sound can we put in front of *out* to make the word *shout*?
- Put *out* back and put *into* in your work space. This word has two little words inside. Cover the last 2 letters and you will see the word *in*. We just said that means the opposite of our word *out*.
- Cover the first 2 letters and you will see the word *to*. This is not how we spell the number two. We would use this *to* in this sentence: *I am going to school*.
- Let's collect our new words and save them to use later in the week.

Day 2: Word Whittle

Distribute the Lesson 11 words and have students place them across the top of their work space. Work through the following sets of clues as described on page 32.

First Word:
1. a word that has the letter *n* in it (*into, funny, down*)
2. a word that has 1 tall letter above the line (*into, funny*)
3. a word that starts with the /f/ sound (*funny*)

Second Word:
1. a word that has 1 syllable (*down, where, that, out*)
2. a word that starts with a consonant (*down, where, that*)
3. a word that fits in this sentence: _____ will we meet after school? (*where*)

Third Word:
1. a word that starts with a consonant (*down, where, funny, that*)
2. a word that starts with 2 consonants in a row (*where, that*)
3. a word that ends with a consonant (*that*)

Fourth Word:
1. a word has an *o* in it (*down, into, out*)
2. a word that has 1 syllable (*down, out*)
3. a word that rhymes with *clown* (*down*)

Have students return the words to the plastic bags and store them for future use.

Day 3: Free Choice Activity Day

Choose one or two of these activities (see pages 18–20):

- [ ] Word Match
- [ ] Word Pop
- [ ] Word Swat
- [ ] Word Sort
- [ ] Voice Choice
- [ ] Cheer the Words
- [ ] Word Detective
- [ ] Rhymer
- [ ] Other: _____

Word Sort

If you choose Word Sort, here are categories that fit this week's words:

- words that end with the same sounds/letters
- words with 3, 4, or 5 letters
- words that relate to place, direction, or location
- words with 1 or 2 syllables

Day 4: Word Builder

Distribute the letter strip of the Lesson 11 Word Card to each student. Have students separate the letters, reviewing the letter names they place them in alphabetical order: *c, e, i, n, s, s,* and *t.*

Have students spell words as you call them out. Write each word on the board as students work and offer a sentence to help them understand its meaning. Call out words in this increasingly difficult order.

in	ice	insect
tin	nice	insects
tins	cent	
	cents	

On the board or in a pocket chart, write the words that contain the spelling pattern *in*; you may also do the same for the *-ice* pattern if your students are ready:

-in	-ice
tin	nice

Have students read over the words in each column. Focus on the *-in* words. Tell students that if they know this pattern, it can help them spell many other words. Invite students to brainstorm

a list of other words that rhyme with *tin*, recording them on the board: *bin, din, fin, kin, pin, win.*

You may repeat this process with *-ice,* if appropriate for your particular students.

To introduce the concept of making plurals, tell students you have something else to show them about the words they made today. Write the following chart on the board: *tin/tins, cent/cents, insect/insects* and explain how to form plurals by adding *s.*

Day 5: Word Smart

Distribute the Lesson 11 words, and ask students to arrange them across the top of their desks, leaving work space below.

Ask students to respond to your questions by picking up the correct word(s) and holding it so that you can see their answers.

Can you find . . .

- a word that starts with the /f/ sound?
- a word that has 2 syllables?
- a word that ends with the /t/ sound? the /n/ sound?
- a word that rhymes with *shout*?
- a word that has a letter that goes below the line?
- a word that has double consonants—or 2 of the same consonants together?
- a word that starts with the /hw/ sound?
- a word that ends with the same sound as the word *bat*?
- a word that means the opposite of *in*? opposite of *up*?
- a word made up of 2 little words?
- a word hiding the little word *do*?
- a word that starts with the same sound as the word *fire*?

* Homework *

Send the letters and words home with each student. Parents can use the words as flash cards and the letters to practice making words, as described in the Parent-Child Word Work sheet.

Day 1: Meet the Words

Pass out the Lesson 12 Word Cards, prepared as described on pages 14–15. Have students break apart the 6 new words and spread them on their desks. Ask students to do the following:

- Hold up each card as you pronounce the word on it.
- Look at the word, read it aloud, and spell it with you.
- Return the word card to the top of their desk.

Then guide students through the following activities, saying:

- Put the word *said* in your work space. We might use *said* in this sentence: *My mother said to clean my room.* That means she was telling me to clean my room.

said

city

citizen

state

little

play

- Put your finger under the letter making the /s/ sound. Put your finger under the last letter that makes the /d/ sound.
- Add the word *city* beside *said.*
- Listen to both words: *city, said.* How do they sound alike? Point to the beginning letter in each that makes the same sound. Sometimes *s* and *c* make the same sound, /s/.
- Put the word *said* back and let's look at *city.* A city is a place where people live. It's the same as a town only bigger. A city has neighborhoods, stores, offices, and a government with a mayor who leads the city. States have lots of towns and cities in them. What are some of the cities in our state?

- *City* has 2 syllables. Let's clap them—*ci-ty.* What letter sounds like *e* at the end? Lots of times *y* represents the long-*e* sound if it's at the end of the word.

- Put the word *citizen* beside *city* in your work space.

- How are these words alike? They have the same first 3 letters.

- Many years ago, *citizen* meant that someone lived in a city rather than in the countryside. That's why it starts with those letters. Now it usually means that someone belongs to a certain state or country. You are a citizen of what state?

- Put *city* back and let's look closer at *citizen.*

- This word has 3 syllables. Let's clap them—*cit-i-zen.*

- This word sounds like it has bees buzzing in it. Listen carefully (stretch out the sounds slowly, emphasizing the /s/ and /z/.)

- You are a citizen of our state of _____. Find the word *state* and put it in your work space.

- A state is made up of many towns and cities and is run by a governor. Our governor is Governor _____.

- Both a city and a state are places that have their own governments to help them run smoothly. Cities and states have many citizens that live in them.

- Cover the first 2 letters of *state,* and you'll find the word *ate.*

- Put these words back and put the word *little* in your work space.

- Take your word *little* and find something in the room that's little, or small, and stand beside it. (Call on students to tell what they found.)

- Come back to your seats and let's trace the word *little* with a finger. It has lots of tall and short letters—up and down like a roller coaster.

- This word has 2 syllables. Let's clap them as we say the word—*lit-tle.* This word has 2 *l*'s and 2 *t*'s.

- Put *little* back and put *play* in your work space.

- *Play* has several meanings. It can be an action verb that means we are having a good time with activities like jumping rope or swinging. Or, *play* can be a noun that means we are acting something out and putting on a show. We could have a play in our classroom for our parents. It can also mean to make music with an instrument, as in play a guitar.

- The first two letters blend together to say /pl/. Can you say that with me? Then we hear a long-*a* sound—/pl/ /ā/. This sound is represented by the letters *a* and *y.* We saw this spelling pattern when we studied *say.* Knowing this pattern can help us spell lots of words!

- Let's collect our new words and save them to use later in the week.

Day 2: Word Whittle

Distribute the Lesson 12 words and have students place them across the top of their work space. Work through the following sets of clues as described on page 32.

First Word:

1. a word that starts with the /s/ sound (*said, city, citizen, state*)
2. a word that has more than 1 syllable (*city, citizens*)
3. a word that is a place (*city*)

Second Word:

1. a word that has the vowel *a* in it (*play, said, state*)
2. a word that has the /ā/ sound (*play, state*)
3. a word that is a place (*state*)

Third Word:

1. a word that has two vowels (*state, little, said*)
2. a word that has two *t*'s (*state, little*)
3. a word that means the opposite of "big" (*little*)

Fourth Word:

1. a word that has one beat or syllable (*said, play, state*)
2. a word with two vowels in it (*said, state*)
3. a word that ends with the letter *d* (*said*)

Day 3: Free Choice Activity Day

Choose one or two of these activities (see pages 18–20):

☐ Word Match   ☐ Word Pop   ☐ Word Swat

☐ Word Sort   ☐ Voice Choice ☐ Cheer the Words

☐ Word Detective ☐ Rhymer   ☐ Other: _____

Word Sort

If you choose Word Sort, here are categories that fit this week's words:

- words that begins with the same sounds/letters

- words with 4, 5, 6, or 7 letters

- words that relate to places

- words with 1, 2, or 3 syllables

- words with long-*a* sound.

Day 4: Word Builder

Distribute the letter strip of the Lesson 12 Word Card to each student. Have students separate the letters, reviewing the letter names as they them in alphabetical order: *a, a, e, l, m, p, t,* and *y.*

Have students spell words as you call them out. Write each word on the board as students work and offer a sentence to help them understand its meaning. Call out words in this order, arranged according to increasing difficulty:

pet	map	lay
met	ate	may
let	mate	pay
lap	late	play
tap	plate	playmate*

* Point out that this is a compound word

On the board or in a pocket chart, sort the written words according to spelling patterns shown below, including *-ate* if desired. Note that *-ap* and *-et* are review patterns (introduced in Word Builder in Weeks 4 and 6) and *-ay* has been discussed in Weeks 10 and 12.

-ap	-et	-ay	-ate
lap	pet	lay	ate
tap	met	may	late
map	let	pay	mate
		play	plate

After you've sorted the words, have students read over the words you've written in each column.

Focus on the *-ay* words. Tell students that if they know this pattern, it can help them spell many other words. Invite students to brainstorm a list of other words that rhyme with *lay*, recording them on the board: *bay, cay, day, hay, ray, say, way.*

You may repeat this process with the other spelling patterns.

Day 5: Word Smart

Distribute the Lesson 12 words, and ask students to arrange them across the top of their desks, leaving work space below.

Ask students to respond to your questions by picking up the correct word(s) and holding it so that you can see their answers. *Can you find . . .*

- a word that starts with the /s/ sound?

- a word that starts the same way as *planet*?

- a word that starts the same way as *stand*?

- a word that rhymes with *late*?

- a word that names a place with a governor for its leader?

- a word that means the opposite of *big*?

- a word that means "tell" or "talk?"

- a word that names a place bigger than a town?

- a word that names a place made up of lots of towns and cities?

- a word that means the opposite of "work?"

- a word that has 2 syllables?

- a word that has 3 syllables?

- a word that fits in this sentence: "Mother _____ not to talk to strangers"?

❋ Homework ❋

Send the letters and words home with each student. Parents can use the words as flash cards and the letters to practice making words, as described in the Parent-Child Word Work sheet.

Day 1: Meet the Words

Pass out the Lesson 13 Word Cards, prepared as described on pages 14–15. Have students break apart the 6 new words and spread them on their desks. Ask students to do the following:

- Hold up each card as you pronounce the word on it.
- Look at the word, read it aloud, and spell it with you.
- Return the word card to the top of their desk.

Then guide students through the following activities, saying:

- Put the word *then* in your work space.
- *Then* is used to indicate the order in which something happens. We might say, "Take out a piece of paper. Then fold it in half."

then

when

I

month

minute

total

- Trace the letter with your fingers. It has a tall letter at the beginning, *t.*
- Put your finger over the *t.* Look! Now we've found a *hen* inside of this word!
- Get the word *when* and put it below the word *then* so that you can see both words.
- What do you notice that both words share? Let's say them both—*when, then.* Yes, they sound alike and have similar spellings with the sound-alike part.
- Put *then* back with the other words, and let's look at *when.*

- Point to the 2 letters that blend to make the /hw/ sound.
- Let's make the /hw/ sound together and put our hand in front of our mouth. Do you feel the air coming from your mouth quickly?
- Put your finger over the first letter. Here's another *hen*!
- Put *when* with the other words and get the word *I.*
- This is a word that we use instead of saying our own names when we talk about ourselves. Instead of saying, "(Your name) wants you to learn this year," I would say, "I want you to learn this year." We have words like this that take the place of names, and we call them pronouns.
- Do you notice that *I* is a word that uses an upper case or capital letter? We must remember to always capitalize that word. We will never use the lower case *i* for that word. (Write both on the board. Cross out the one that is never used.)
- Let's use *I* in a sentence. Turn to your buddy and say, "I like to _____" and tell them something you enjoy doing.

- Put the word *I* back and get *month.*
- Months help us keep up with units of time. There are 12 months in a year. What month are we in now? What month is your birthday in? (Allow several students to share.)
- Point to the letter that makes the /m/ sound at the beginning.
- Let's clap the beats in this word: *month.* There's one syllable in this word.
- Find the word *minute* and put it beside *month.* Both of these are time words. Which word represents the longer amount of time? Which word represents the shorter amount of time? A minute is made up of 60 seconds. Let's look at the clock and see just how long a minute is.
- Point to the letter in *minute* that represents the /t/ sound.
- Let's clap the beats in this word: *min-ute.* This word has two syllables. Put both *minute* and *month* back with the other words. Get the word *total.*
- *Total* means everything together. If I give you a cookie and then another cookie, the total number of cookies would be two. Yum!
- Take your finger and trace across the top of this word, It goes up, down, up, down, up–like a roller coaster!
- Point to the letters that make the /t/ sound. Yes, they are at the beginning and middle of the word.
- Let's collect our new words and save them to use later in the week.

Day 2: Word Whittle

Distribute the Lesson 13 words and have students place them across the top of their work space. Work through the following sets of clues as described on page 32.

First Word:
1. a word that has a *t* in it (*then, month, minute, total*)
2. a word that has an *o* in it (*month, total*)
3. a word that fits in this sentence: I was born in the _____ of September. (*month*)

Second Word:
1. a word that has one syllable (*then, I, month, when*)
2. words that sound alike or rhyme (*then, when*)
3. a word that starts with this sound–/hw/ (*when*)

Third Word:
1. a word that has the vowel *e* in it (*then, when, minute*)
2. a word that has the little word *hen* inside (*then, when*)

3. a word that makes your tongue touch your top teeth when you say it (*then*)

Fourth Word:

1. a word that has one vowel in it (*then, when, month, I*)
2. a word that does not have the letter *t* in it (*when, I*)
3. a word that has fewer than 4 letters (*I*)

Day 3: Free Choice Activity Day

Choose one or two of these activities (see pages 18–20):

☐ Word Match ☐ Word Pop ☐ Word Swat

☐ Word Sort ☐ Voice Choice ☐ Cheer the Words

☐ Word Detective ☐ Rhymer ☐ Other: _____

Word Sort

If you choose Word Sort, here are categories that fit this week's words:

- words that begins with the same sounds/letters.
- words with 4 or 5 letters
- words that relate to time
- words that rhyme
- words with 1 or 2 syllables
- words with short-*e* sound
- words with blends

Day 4: Word Builder

Distribute the letter strip of the Lesson 13 Word Card to each student. Have students separate the letters, reviewing the letter names as they place them in alphabetical order: *e, i, m, n, s, t,* and *u.*

Have students spell words as you call them out. Write each word on the board as students work, and offer a sentence to help them understand its meaning. Call out words in this order, arranged according to increasing difficulty, including the shaded words if your students are ready:

in	met	nut	*menu*
tin	set	nuts	*menus*
sin	net	*must*	*minute*
me	nets	*men*	*minutes*

On the board or in a pocket chart, sort the written words according to spelling patterns, as shown below.

-in	-et
in	met
tin	set
sin	net

After you've sorted the words, have students read over the words in each column. Note that both of these patterns are review.

Focus on the *-in* words. Tell students that if they know this pattern, it can help them spell many other words. Invite students to brainstorm a list of other words that rhyme with *in*, recording them on the board: *bin, din, fin, kin, pin, tin, win, thin, grin, chin*. Repeat this process with *-et.*

You may also want to review how to form plurals with the words from this week: *net/nets, nut/nuts, menu/menus, minute/minutes.*

Day 5: Word Smart

Distribute the Lesson 13 words, and ask students to arrange them across the top of their desks, leaving work space below.

Ask students to respond to your questions by picking up the correct word(s) and holding it so that you can see their answers. *Can you find . . .*

- two words that rhyme?
- a word with 2 *t*'s? with the /hw/ sound?
- a word hiding a *hen*? (*when, then*)
- a word that is always written in capital letters?
- a word with the /th/ sound?
- a word with 1 tall letter? the vowel *o* in it?
- a word that has 2 syllables?
- a word that there are 12 of in a year? 60 of in one hour?
- a word that takes the place of your name when you talk?
- a word with 3 tall letters?
- a word hiding something a squirrel might like to eat?

✳ Homework ✳

Send the letters and words home with each student. Parents can use the words as flash cards and the letters to practice making words, as described in the Parent-Child Word Work sheet.

Day 1: Meet the Words

Pass out the Lesson 14 Word Cards, prepared as described on pages 14–15. Have students break apart the 6 new words and spread them on their desks. Ask students to do the following:

- Hold up each card as you pronounce the word on it.
- Look at the word, read it aloud, and spell it with you.
- Return the word card to the top of their desk.

Then guide students through the following activities, saying:

- Put the word *you* in your work space.
- This word is used in the sentence, *Will you take the dog for a walk?* It's a word that stands for the person we're talking to, just as the word *I* stands for yourself when you're talking. Both *you* and *I* are called pronouns.

you

too

red

look

how

year

- Notice that the word has three letters, but when we say the word it is the name of one letter in our alphabet. Let's say it–*you*. The letter it names is in this word. Can you point to the letter?
- Find the word *too* and put it beside *you*. Do you hear how these words rhyme–*too, you*? They are spelled differently, but they sound alike. Sometimes the same sound can be spelled in different ways.
- Put *you* back and let's look at *too*. There are several different words that are pronounced /tōo/. One is the number two, but it is spelled *t-w-o*. T-o-o means *also*. I might say, *Let's buy some watermelon and some peaches, too.* It's the same as saying, *Let's buy some watermelon and some peaches, also.*
- Put you finger under the letter that makes the /t/ sound.
- Let's put *too* back and get *red*.
- *R-e-d* is the color. There is another word pronounced the same way–*read*. (Write this on the board.) I might say, *We've read many books this year.* There are some words we'll find that sound alike but have different spellings and meanings, such as *two* the number and *too* that means "also." They are called *homophones*.
- This word has three sounds. Put your finger under each letter as I make its sound–/r/, /e/, /d/.
- Pick up your word and quickly stand up and find something in the room that is red. Put your word on it and wait to be called on. (Allow students to share quickly what they have found.)

- Put your finger over the *r* in the word. If I changed the *r* to an *f*, it would read *fed*. If I put an *l* there, it would read *led*.
- Put *red* back and get *look*. The two *o*'s in the middle look like eyes that are looking, don't they?
- Put your finger under the letter that makes the /l/ sound.
- There are 2 letters making the /ŏŏ/ sound. Put your fingers under those letters.
- Now put your finger under the letter that makes the /k/ sound.
- Put your finger over the *l*. If I put a *b* there instead, the word would be *book*. If I put a *t* at the beginning, it would be *took*. These patterns help us spell more words.
- Put *look* back and get *how*. *How* describes the way something is done: *I know how to tie my shoes.* It's often used to ask a question: *How do you get to school in the morning?*
- Trace the word with your finger. It has a tall letter at the beginning.
- Let's clap the beats in this word: *how*. It has one beat.
- Put *how* back and get the word *year*.
- *Year* is a measurement of time. There are 52 weeks in a year. There are 365 days in a year. It's how we measure our birthdays to tell how old we are.
- Put your finger over the *y*. Now the word spells *ear*. Touch your ear. Now let's put those sounds together: *year*.
- Cover the first letter with your finger. If I put a *t* at the beginning, I would have *tear*. If I put an *f* there, I would have *fear*. What would I have if I put a *d* there?
- Let's collect our new words and save them to use later in the week.

Day 2: Word Whittle

Distribute the Lesson 14 words and have students place them across the top of their work space. Work through the following sets of clues as described on page 32.

First Word:
1. a word that has the vowel *o* in it (*you, look, how, too*)
2. a word that has tall letters in it (*look, how, too*)
3. a word that rhymes with *brook* (*look*)

Second Word:
1. a word that has more than 1 vowel (*you, look, too, year*)
2. a word with a letter that falls below the line (*you, year*)
3. a word that equals 52 weeks (*year*)

Third Word:
1. a word that ends with a consonant (*look, how, red, year*)

2. a word that has 1 vowel (*how, red*)
3. a word that names a color (*red*)

Fourth Word:

1. a word that has 3 letters (*you, how, red, too*)
2. a word that has at least one *o* in it (*you, how, too*)
3. a word that means "also" (*too*)

Day 3: Free Choice Activity Day

Choose one or two of these activities (see pages 18–20):

- [ ] Word Match
- [ ] Word Pop
- [ ] Word Swat
- [ ] Word Sort
- [ ] Voice Choice
- [ ] Cheer the Words
- [ ] Word Detective
- [ ] Rhymer
- [ ] Other: _____

Word Sort

If you choose Word Sort, here are categories that fit this week's words:

- words that begin with the same sounds or letters
- words with 3 or 4 letters
- words that rhyme
- words with 1 syllable
- words with 1 or 2 vowels

Day 4: Word Builder

Distribute the letter strip of the Lesson 14 Word Card to each student. Have students separate the letters, reviewing the letter names as they place them in alphabetical order: *a, a, c, d, e l, n,* and *r.*

Have students spell words as you call them out. Write each word on the board as students work and offer a sentence to help them understand its meaning. Call out words in this order, arranged according to increasing difficulty, including the shaded words if your students are ready:

car	Dan*	lane	race
care	ran	cane	calendar
dare	and	end	
can	land	lend	

* Point out that names always begin with a capital letter.

Remind the students that a calendar helps us keep track of the *year*, which is one of the weekly words. It has 12 months and 52 weeks.

On the board or in a pocket chart, sort the written words according to spelling patterns, using as many as your students are ready for; *-an* is a review pattern.

-an	-end	-are	-and	-ane
can	end	care	and	lane
ran	lend	dare	land	cane
Dan				

After you've sorted the words, have students read over the words in each column.

Focus on the *-end* words. Tell students that if they know this pattern, it can help them spell many other words. Invite students to brainstorm a list of other words that rhyme with *end*, recording them on the board: *bend, fend, lend, mend, send, tend.*

Repeat this process for *-an* if you'd like to review it with your students, and with the other spelling patterns if desired.

Day 5: Word Smart

Distribute the Lesson 14 words, and ask students to arrange them across the top of their desks, leaving work space below.

Ask students to respond to your questions by picking up the correct word(s) and holding it so that you can see their answers. *Can you find . . .*

- two words that rhyme? that have double vowels?
- a word that rhymes with *bed?*
- a word that rhymes with *shoe?*
- a word that starts and ends with a tall letter?
- a word that means "also"?
- a word that is the color of a candy apple?
- a word that fits in this sentence: "Will you help me _____ for my lost dog?"
- a word with only 1 vowel?
- a word that fits in this sentence: "Can _____ come outside and play?"
- a word that sounds like the name of one letter of the alphabet?
- a word that equals 12 months?

✳ Homework ✳

Send the letters and words home with each student. Parents can use the words as flash cards and the letters to practice making words, as described in the Parent-Child Word Work sheet.

Lesson 15

Day 1: Meet the Words

Pass out the Lesson 15 Word Cards, prepared as described on pages 14–15. Have students break apart the 6 new words and spread them on their desks. Ask students to do the following:

- Hold up each card as you pronounce the word on it.
- Look at the word, read it aloud, and spell it with you.
- Return the word card to the top of their desk.

Then guide students through the following activities, saying:

- Put the word *we* in your work space.
- *We* is what we call a pronoun, a word that takes the place of names. Instead of saying, "Sally, Tom, and I are going to the store," you could say, "We are going to the store." We've studied other pronouns: *I* and *you*. *He* and *she* are pronouns, too.

we

for

can't

down

come

light

- Put your finger under the letter that's making the /w/ sound.
- Put your finger under the letter that makes the long-e sound. Do you hear the letter say its own name?
- Put *we* back and get the word *for*. This word sounds just like the number four, but it isn't that word. This word is used in this sentence: *I am working for the school.* Words that sound alike but have different meanings and spellings are called homophones. We studied *too* last week, a word that also sounds like a number, *two*. (Write the words on the board as you say them.)
- Point to the letter that makes the /f/ sound.
- Now cover the first letter, *f*, with your finger. The word *or* is hiding there. We use *or* to give a choice: Would you like the red apple or the yellow apple? Put *for* back and get the word *can't*.
- This word has a different little mark than most of our words. The mark is called an apostrophe.
- We use an apostrophe with some words to show that there are some missing letters. *Can't* means "can not." Instead of writing or saying *can not*, we sometimes use a word that isn't so fancy and that sounds more like our everyday language. We say "can't." This combines *can* and *not*—pushing them together, leaving out the second *n* and *o*, putting in an apostrophe and ending with *t*. (Demonstrate by writing *can not* on the board and showing how the apostrophe joins the two words and stands in for the missing letters.)

- Let's touch and spell this one together. When we come to the apostrophe, let's make a click with our mouths. "C-a-n-*click*-t."
- I might use *can't* in this sentence: *Let's help Joey because he can't find his dog.* Put back *can't* and get the word *down*.
- The opposite of *down* is *up*. Can you reach up towards the sky? Now down and touch the floor?
- Put your finger under the first letter that makes the /d/ sound.
- Find the 2 letters that combine to represent the /ou/ sound.
- Point to the letter that makes the /n/ sound.
- The words *town*, *clown*, and *frown* rhyme with *down* and are spelled with the same *-own* pattern. If we know *down*, we can spell so many other words.
- Use your fingers to cover the last 2 letters. The little word *do* is hiding there. *I do like chocolate ice cream!*
- Put back the word *down* and get *come*.
- Touch the letter at the beginning that represents the /k/ sound. The letter *k* also represents that sound.
- Now touch the letter that makes the /m/ sound.
- Put your finger over the first 2 letters, and you'll find *me* hiding there! Put *come* back and get the word *light*.
- We have light that is manmade, such as the light that comes from a flashlight or a light bulb, and we have light that is natural, like the light that comes from the sun. Sunlight can warm us, and all light helps us see.
- Now trace the word with your fingers. This word has three letters that go above the line and one letter that goes below the line. It's like a roller coaster!
- Let's collect our new words and save them to use later in the week.

Day 2: Word Whittle

Distribute the Lesson 15 words and have students place them across the top of their work space. Work through the following sets of clues as described on page 32.

First Word:
1. a word that has the vowel *o* in it (*for, down, come*)
2. a word that has four letters (*down, come*)
3. a word that starts with a tall letter (*down*)

Second Word:
1. a word that starts with a letter that doesn't go above or below the line (*we, come, can't*)

2. a word that has the vowel e in it (we, come)
3. a word that is a pronoun that takes the place of names (we)

Third Word:
1. a word that has a tall letter in it (can't, down, light, for)
2. a word that ends with a t (can't, light)
3. a word that is a contraction (can't)

Fourth Word:
1. a word that has four letters (can't, down, come)
2. a word that starts with the sound /k/ (can't, come)
3. a word that rhymes with some (come)

Day 3: Free Choice Activity Day

Choose one or two of these activities (see pages 18–20):

☐ Word Match   ☐ Word Pop   ☐ Word Swat
☐ Word Sort   ☐ Voice Choice   ☐ Cheer the Words
☐ Word Detective ☐ Rhymer   ☐ Other: _____

Word Sort

If you choose Word Sort, here are categories that fit this week's words:

- words that begins with the same sounds or letters
- words with 3 or 4 letters
- words with 1 syllable
- words with 1 or 2 vowels
- words with silent letters

Day 4: Word Builder

Distribute the letter strip of the Lesson 15 Word Card to each student. Have students separate the letters, reviewing the letter names they place them in alphabetical order: c, e, m, o, p, r, t and u.

Have students spell words as you call them out. Write each word on the board as students work and offer a sentence to help them understand its meaning. Call out words in this increasingly difficult order, including the shaded words if your students are ready:

me	cop	pot	more
met	top	put	core
pet	mop	cute	come
up	rot	mute	computer
cup	cot	tore	

On the board or in a pocket chart, sort the written words according to spelling patterns shown below, including -ute and -ore if your students are ready. (Note that -et, -op, and -ot are review patterns.)

-et	-up	-op	-ot	-ute	-ore
met	up	cop	rot	cute	tore
pet	cup	top	cot	mute	more
		mop	pot		core

After you've sorted the words, have students read over the words in each column.

Focus on the -up words. Tell students that if they know this pattern, it can help them spell other words. Invite students to brainstorm a list of other words that rhyme with up, recording them on the board: cup, pup, sup.

You may repeat this process with the other spelling patterns as appropriate for your particular students.

Day 5: Word Smart

Distribute the Lesson 15 words, and ask students to arrange them across the top of their desks, leaving work space below.

Ask students to respond to your questions by picking up the correct word(s) and holding it so that you can see their answers. *Can you find . . .*

- a word that starts with the same sound as candy?
- a word that starts with the sound /f/?
- a word that starts with the sound /d/?
- a word that rhymes with fight?
- a word that rhymes with clown?
- a word that rhymes with me?
- a word that ends with the /t/ sound?
- a word that has an apostrophe in it?
- a word that means the opposite of up?
- a word that is hiding the little word me?
- a word that is hiding the little word do?
- a word that is a contraction?
- a word that fits in this sentence: "Don't ever say you _____ do something until you try it"?
- a word that takes the place of people's names?

❋ Homework ❋

Send the letters and words home with each student. Parents can use the words as flash cards and the letters to practice making words, as described in the Parent-Child Word Work sheet.

Day 1: Meet the Words

Pass out the Lesson 16 Word Cards, prepared as described on pages 14–15. Have students break apart the 6 new words and spread them on their desks. Ask students to do the following:

- Hold up each card as you pronounce the word on it.
- Look at the word, read it aloud, and spell it with you.
- Return the word card to the top of their desk.

Then guide students through the following activities, saying:

- Put the word *up* in your work space.
- *Up* means the opposite of *down*. Let's reach down to the floor with our hands. Now let's reach up to the ceiling.

up

see

my

yellow

on

question

- Put your finger under the letter that's making the /u/ sound, the vowel *u*. Put your finger under the letter that makes the /p/ sound, the letter *p*.
- Make a *c* with your thumb and index finger on your left hand. Put your *c* in front of the word *up*. Now, we've spelled the word *cup*!
- Put *up* away and get the word *see*.
- Use your eyes to look around the room and tell me something that you see. (Call on a few students to share what they see.)
- Put your finger under the letter that makes the /s/ sound.

- Point to the 2 *e*'s. Together they represent the long-*e* sound, /ē/. So we have 3 letters in this word, but only 2 sounds—/s/ and /ē/.
- Put *see* away and get the word *my*. *My* is a word that shows that something belongs to you, like "This is my pencil."
- Turn to a neighbor and tell him or her about something that belongs to you that you love. Be sure to use the word *my*.
- Point your finger to the letter that represents /m/, the *m*.
- The next sound is /ī/, but what letter do you see? It's a *y*, not an *i*. There's more than one way to write the /ī/ sound, which we call the long-*i* sound.
- Put *my* away and get the word *yellow*. Yellow is a color. Take your word that says "yellow" and find something in the room that is yellow. Stand beside it with your word. (Call on students to tell what they found.)
- Take your seats and let's trace around this word with our finger,

going up around the tall letters and down low around the tail of the *y*.

- Put your finger under the first letter that represents /y/.
- Point to the double *ll*'s in the word.
- We hear the long-*o* sound at the end of *yellow*. Let's look at how it's spelled. Two letters represent the /ō/ sound in this word: *o* and *w*. Sometimes two letters represent one sound.
- Put *yellow* away and get the little word *on*.
- This is a word we use a lot in our reading, writing, and speaking. We might turn on the light and then turn it off. (Send a student to the light switch to demonstrate.) What are some other things we turn on? (Invite responses.) I might step on the mat, then off it. (Demonstrate.) I might put a book on the desk. (Demonstrate.)
- Let's count the letters and sounds in this word. (Count.) There are two letters, and two sounds. In this word, each letter represents one sound. Put *on* back and get the word *question*.
- A question is something we ask when we want information. We might ask each other questions–things we want to know about each other. (Ask one student a question such as, "Do you have a pet?" or "How old are you?")
- Now I have another question for you: Do you have a good friend? I'll bet you're together with your friend often. When you see the letter *q*, you will always see its good friend *u* alongside it. (Write a few *q* words on the board–*queen, quick, quack*. Underline the *qu*–*q* and its good friend *u*.) Now put your fingers under these 2 letters that represent the /kw/ sound.
- There are some other letters in this word that are good friends. You won't always see them together, but they'll be together often. Run your finger under the letters *t-i-o-n*. Listen to how these letters sound when they're together–/shun/.
- Now, turn to a friend and ask them a question about themselves so that you can get to know them better.
- Let's collect our new words and save them to use later in the week.

Day 2: Word Whittle

Distribute the Lesson 16 words and have students place them across the top of their work space. Work through the following sets of clues as described on page 32.

First Word:
1. a word that has the vowel *o* in it (*yellow, on, question*)
2. a word that has at least one tall letter (*yellow, question*)
3. a word that has 2 of the same letters in it (*yellow*)

Second Word:
1. a word that has just one syllable (*up, see, my, on*)
2. a word that starts with a vowel (*up, on*)
3. a word that rhymes with *pup* (*up*)

Third Word:
1. a word that has a letter that goes below the line (*up, my, yellow, question*)
2. a word that begins or ends in *y* (*my, yellow*)
3. a word with fewer than 6 letters (*my*)

Fourth Word:
1. a word that has more than 2 letters in it (*see, yellow, question*)
2. a word that has 2 syllables (*yellow, question*)
3. a word that shows that you want some information or you want to learn something (*question*)

Day 3: Free Choice Activity Day

Choose one or two of these activities (see pages 18–20):

☐ Word Match ☐ Word Pop ☐ Word Swat

☐ Word Sort ☐ Voice Choice ☐ Cheer the Words

☐ Word Detective ☐ Rhymer ☐ Other: _____

Word Sort
If you choose Word Sort, here are categories that fit this week's words:

- words with 2 letters
- words with 1 or 2 syllables
- words with 1 or 2 vowels
- words with tall letters
- words with letters below the line

Day 4: Word Builder

Distribute the letter strip of the Lesson 16 Word Card to each student. Have students separate the letters, reviewing the letter names as they place them in alphabetical order: *e, i, n, o, q, s, s, t,* and *u*.

Have students spell words as you call them out. Write each word on the board as students work and offer a sentence to help them understand its meaning. Call out words in this increasingly difficult order, including the shaded words if your students are ready:

in	quit	tunes	nests
tin	son	toe	quest
ten	ton	toes	question
it	tons	nose	questions
sit	tune	nest	

On the board or in a pocket chart, sort the written words according to spelling patterns shown below, including -*est* if your students are ready:

-in	-it	-on	-est
in	sit	ton	nest
tin	quit	son	quest

After you've sorted the words, have students read over the words in each column.

Focus on the -*it* words. Tell students that if they know this pattern, it can help them spell many other words. Invite students to brainstorm a list of other words that rhyme with *sit*, recording them on the board: *bit, fit, hit, kit, lit, knit, pit, quit, wit.*

You may repeat this process with the other spelling patterns.

You may want to review the concept of forming plurals by adding an -*s* to the ends of words: *tin/tins, ton/tons, tune/tunes, toe/toes, nest/nests.*

Day 5: Word Smart

Distribute the Lesson 16 words, and ask students to arrange them across the top of their desks, leaving work space below.

Ask students to respond to your questions by picking up the correct word(s) and holding it so that you can see their answers. *Can you find . . .*

- a word that rhymes with *cup*?
- a word that rhymes with a little insect that buzzes?
- a word that is a color? has 2 of the same letter?
- a word hiding the word *low* in it?
- a word that starts with the sound /kw/?
- a word that starts with the same sound *snake* does?
- a word that has the vowel *u* in it? with a long-*e* sound?
- a word that means the opposite of *down*?
- a word where *y* represents the /ī/ sound?
- a word that fits in this sentence: "Did you ask me a _____?"
- a word that has one of our other words inside of it?
- a word that would be a pet if you added a *p* to the beginning?

❋ Homework ❋

Send the letters and words home with each student. Parents can use the words as flash cards and the letters to practice making words, as described in the Parent-Child Word Work sheet.

Day 1: Meet the Words

Pass out the Lesson 17 Word Cards, prepared as described on pages 14–15. Have students break apart the 6 new words and spread them on their desks. Ask students to do the following:

- Hold up each card as you pronounce the word on it.
- Look at the word, read it aloud, and spell it with you.
- Return the word card to the top of their desk.

Then guide students through the following activities, saying:

- Put the word *go* in your work space. Put your finger under the letter that represents the /g/ sound. Put your finger under the letter that represents the long-*o* sound, /ō/.

go

do

one

big

plant

planet

- Put the word *do* beside the word *go*. You would think that they would rhyme, but they don't. The *o* in each word represents a different sound. Listen as I say each of them slowly. (Pronounce them.) One *o* represents the long-*o* sound, which is the same as its name–*go*. The other *o* has a different sound–/o͞o/

- Both of these words are verbs. They show action: *We go to town. We do our best. I go to the office. You do your homework.* They're little words, but they are mighty!

- Put those words back and get the word *one*.

- Cover the *e* with your finger. Now we have the little word *on*, which we studied last week.

- This word is pronounced exactly like the word *won*. (Write both on the board.) These words are homophones, just like *two* and *too* and *four* and *for*. Just like the other homophone pairs we've studied, the first word, *o-n-e*, refers to a number. *W-o-n* means you came in first at a game or race. We sometimes have to know how a word is used before we can spell it correctly.

- Put *one* back and get the word *big*.

- Put your finger under the letter representing the sounds that I say–/b/, /i/, /g/. This word has three letters and three sounds.

- The pattern *-ig* is an important one for us to know. If we know the word *big*, it can help us read and write many new words such *pig*, *fig*, *twig*, *dig*, *rig*, and *wig*.

- What are some words that you can think of that can be used instead of the word *big*? (*gigantic, monstrous, huge, large, enormous*, and so on) These are all synonyms for *big*. We want to

remember to use as many different descriptive words as we can in our writing.

- Put away *big* and get the words *plant* and *planet*. Look how adding one little letter *e* to *plant* changes it from something tiny like a flower into a gigantic planet like the one we live on–Earth!

- Put the word *planet* below the word *plant*. Notice how they both start with *p-l*. /P/ and /l/ blend together to make the sound /pl/. Let's say that together, /pl/. This sound is in many words, such as *play, plenty, plan,* and *please*.

- The word *plant* has a little tiny insect inside of it. Do you see an ant? Cover the *p* and *l* and you will! We have an ant in our plant! That rhymes!

- *Plant* has a couple of different meanings. It can mean to put seeds in the ground to grow something. "I am going to plant the flowers." Or, it can be the thing that grows from those seeds. "My tomato plant is growing tall."

- Now look at *planet*. Earth is one of the planets in our solar system. Planets orbit or revolve around the sun. Can you name some of the planets?

- Let's collect our new words and save them to use later in the week.

Day 2: Word Whittle

Distribute the Lesson 17 words and have students place them across the top of their work space. Work through the following sets of clues as described on page 32.

First Word:
1. a word that has an *o* in it (*go, one, do*)
2. a word that is a verb that tells us something is happening or that there is action (*go, do*)
3. a word that has a vowel that says its own name, /ō/ (*go*)

Second Word:
1. a word that starts with a consonant (*go, big, do, plant, planet*)
2. a word that does not have an *o* in it (*big, plant, planet*)
3. a word that has a little insect hiding inside of it (*plant*)

Third Word:
1. a word that has letters that go below the line (*go, big, plant, planet*)
2. a word that starts with the same sound the word *play* starts with (*plant, planet*)
3. a word that has 2 syllables (*planet*)

Fourth Word:
1. a word that ends with vowel (*go, do, one*)

2. a word with two letters (*go, do*)
3. a word that rhymes with *moo* (*do*)

Day 3: Free Choice Activity Day

Choose one or two of these activities (see pages 18–20):

☐ Word Match ☐ Word Pop ☐ Word Swat

☐ Word Sort ☐ Voice Choice ☐ Cheer the Words

☐ Word Detective ☐ Rhymer ☐ Other: _____

Word Sort

If you choose Word Sort, here are categories that fit this week's words:

- words with 2 or 3 letters
- words with 1 or 2 syllables
- words with /n/ sound
- words with 1 or 2 vowels
- words with tall letters
- words with letters below the line

Day 4: Word Builder

Distribute the letter strip of the Lesson 17 Word Card to each student. Have students separate the letters, reviewing the letter names as they place them in alphabetical order: *a, d, e, g, n, r,* and, *s.*

Have students spell words as you call them out. Write each word on the board as students work and offer a sentence to help them understand its meaning. Call out words in this increasingly difficult order, including the shaded words if desired:

an	rang	*read*
ran	sang	end
sag	*gas*	send
nag	*dear*	*grand*
rag	*dare*	*gardens*
snag	red	

On the board or in a pocket chart, sort the written words according to the spelling patterns below, including -*ang* if your students are ready:

-an	-ag	-end	-ang
an	sag	end	*rang*
ran	nag	send	*sang*
	rag		
	snag		

After you've sorted the words, have students read over the words in each column.

Focus on the -*ag* words. Tell students that if they know this pattern, it can help them spell many other words. Invite students to brainstorm a list of other words that rhyme with *sag*, recording them on the board and providing definitions as necessary: *bag, gag, nag, jag, lag, nag, rag, tag, wag, zag, brag, drag, snag, stag.*

You may repeat this process with the other spelling patterns.

You may want to quickly review homophones: *one/on, two/too, four/for, red/read.*

Day 5: Word Smart

Distribute the Lesson 17 words, and ask students to arrange them across the top of their desks, leaving work space below.

Ask students to respond to your questions by picking up the correct word(s) and holding it so that you can see their answers.

Can you find . . .

- a word that begins with /d/?
- a word that begins with /b/?
- a word that ends with /t/?
- a word that rhymes with *wig*?
- a word that rhymes with *fun*?
- a word that means the opposite of *small*?
- a word that means the opposite of *stop*?
- a word that has 2 tall letters?
- a word without any tall letters?
- a word that means the same as *huge* or *enormous*?
- a word that fits in this expression: "Get ready. Get Set. ____!"?
- a word that has an insect hiding inside?
- a word that starts many question sentences?
- a word that rhymes with *chant, pant,* and *grant*?
- a word with the little word *on* hiding inside?

✳ Homework ✳

Send the letters and words home with each student. Parents can use the words as flash cards and the letters to practice making words, as described in the Parent-Child Word Work sheet.

Day 1: Meet the Words

Pass out the Lesson 18 Word Cards, prepared as described on pages 14–15. Have students break apart the 6 new words and spread them on their desks. Ask students to do the following:

- Hold up each card as you pronounce the word on it.
- Look at the word, read it aloud, and spell it with you.
- Return the word card to the top of their desk.

Then guide students through the following activities, saying:

- Put the word *make* in your work space.
- Point to the letters that represent these sounds in the word: /m/, /ā/, /k/.

make

away

blue

here

think

unit

- Now put your finger under the *e*. That letter is silent. Most often *e* is silent if it comes at the end of a word.
- Put your finger under the letter that I would have to change to make this word into *bake*. Yes, I would have to change the *m* to a *b*.
- The *-ake* pattern can help us spell many words. We can use it to help us spell *fake, take, Jake, rake, flake*, and many other words.
- Put *make* with the other words and get the word *away*. This word starts with the vowel *a*. Put your finger under it. Point to the letter that makes the /w/ sound, the *w*.
- This word has another important pattern. Cover the first 2 letters. *A* and *y* are left. They represent the sound /ā/ and can help us spell many other words, like *say, bay, may,* and *tray*.
- Return *away* and get the word *blue*. This word names a color.
- Sometimes people who are sad say that they are blue. Why do you think they use that color word to describe how they feel?
- Put your finger under the first 2 letters—*b-l*. Together those blend to make the sound /bl/. This is the same sound as the beginning of *blood, blouse,* and *blog.*
- Blue is one of our primary colors. If we mix blue and yellow, we get green! Put *blue* back and get *here*.
- This is another word that has a homophone—a word that is pronounced the same but has different meaning and spelling. This *here* means a place. We might say, *Come here.* Or *Here is where I want to plant the tree.* The other *hear* (write this) means to listen.

(Underline the *ear* in that word.) The little word *ear* can help us to remember that this one is the one that means to use our ears.

- Cover the last letter, *e*. Now the word says *her*, as in *I like her dress.* Cover the last 2 letters, *r* and *e*. Now we have *he*, as in *He is 6 years old.* Two people are hiding in this little word—*her* and *he*!
- Put that word back and get *think.* Cover the *i-n-k.*
- The 2 letters left represent the /th/ sound. That's the same sound as in *thank* and *thin.*
- Cover the first 2 letters. Now we have the word *ink*. We write with ink. And we can use this pattern to spell other words, such as *sink, pink, drink.* Point to the letter that makes the /k/ sound, the *k*.
- Put *think* back and get *unit.*
- Put your finger on the first letter. It says its own name /ū/. Often words that start with *u-n* are pronounced /un/, but this one is not.
- Put your finger under the letter that makes the /n/ sound, the *n*.
- Cover the first 2 letters. Now we have the word *it.*
- This is a word we use a lot in math. Sometimes we measure using units. (Demonstrate.) We might connect these cubes (use whatever you have available) to measure the length of this pencil. If I connect 8 cubes, I might say that this pencil is 8 units long.
- There is another meaning for this word, too. Many of the books we use in this class are grouped into what we call units. In our reading book, all of the animal stories are in one unit. Units are a way of organizing ideas.
- Let's collect our new words and save them to use later in the week.

Day 2: Word Whittle

Distribute the Lesson 18 words and have students place them across the top of their work space. Work through the following sets of clues as described on page 32.

First Word:

1. a word that has at least 1 tall letter (*blue, here, make, think, unit*)
2. a word that has the vowel *e* at the end (*blue, here, make*)
3. a word that names a color (*blue*)

Second Word:

1. a word that starts with a consonant (*blue, here, make, think*)
2. a word that has at least 2 tall letters (*blue, think*)
3. a word that rhymes with *wink* (*think*)

Third Word:

1. a word that has 2 vowels (*blue, away, here, make*)

2. a word that ends with the vowel *e* (*blue, here, make*)
3. a word that can help us spell *bake* (*make*)

Fourth Word:

1. a word that has 2 vowels (*blue, here, away, make, unit*)
2. a word that has 2 of the same vowel (*away, here*)
3. a word that has 2 syllables (*away*)

Day 3: Free Choice Activity Day

Choose one or two of these activities (see pages 18–20):

☐ Word Match   ☐ Word Pop   ☐ Word Swat

☐ Word Sort   ☐ Voice Choice   ☐ Cheer the Words

☐ Word Detective   ☐ Rhymer   ☐ Other: _____

Word Sort

If you choose Word Sort, here are categories that fit this week's words:

- words with 1 syllable
- words with tall letters
- words with silent *e*
- words with 2 vowels
- words with *a*'s
- words with *e*'s

Day 4: Word Builder

Distribute the letter strip of the Lesson 18 Word Card to each student. Have students separate the letters, reviewing the letter names as they place them in alphabetical order: *e, c, i, p, r, s, t,* and *u.*

Have students spell words as you call them out. Write each word on the board as students work and offer a sentence to help them understand its meaning. Call out words in this increasingly difficult order, including the shaded words if your students are ready:

it	tip	cups	tires
sit	tips	put	site
pit	pie	cut	spite
pits	pies	cute	sprite
spit	up	cuter	picture
sip	cup	tire	pictures

On the board or in a pocket chart, sort the written words according to spelling patterns as shown below.

-it	-ip	-ite
sit	sip	site
pit	tip	spite
spit		sprite

After you've sorted the words, have students read over the words in each column.

Focus on the *-ip* words. Tell students that if they know this pattern, it can help them spell many other words. Invite students to brainstorm a list of other words that rhyme with *sip*, recording them on the board: *dip, hip, lip, nip, rip, tip, zip, ship, chip, slip, blip, flip, trip, grip.*

You may repeat this process with the other spelling patterns, as appropriate for your particular students.

Day 5: Word Smart

Distribute the Lesson 18 words, and ask students to arrange them across the top of their desks, leaving work space below.

Ask students to respond to your questions by picking up the correct word(s) and holding it so that you can see their answers.
Can you find . . .

- a word that starts with the blend /bl/?
- a word that starts with a vowel?
- a word that starts with the sound /th/?
- a word that ends with the /t/ sound?
- a word that rhymes with *shoe*?
- a word that rhymes with *say*?
- a word that is used to measure in math?
- a word that is hiding the word *her*?
- a word that is hiding the word *it*?
- a word that is hiding the word *ink*?
- a word that is hiding the word *he*?
- a word that has 2 syllables?
- a word that some people use to describe a sad mood?
- a word that fits in this sentence: "Mixing yellow and _____ makes green"?
- a word that fits in this sentence: "Don't wander _____ from your parents in a store"?

✳ Homework ✳

Send the letters and words home with each student. Parents can use the words as flash cards and the letters to practice making words, as described in the Parent-Child Word Work sheet.

Day 1: Meet the Words

Pass out the Lesson 19 Word Cards, prepared as described on pages 14–15. Have students break apart the 6 new words and spread them on their desks. Ask students to do the following:

- Hold up each card as you pronounce the word on it.
- Look at the word, read it aloud, and spell it with you.
- Return the word card to the top of their desk.

Then guide students through the following activities, saying:

- Put the word *run* in your work space.
- *Run* is something we might do on the playground but probably not in our classroom. Machines run, too, but they run in a different way. For machines, running would mean that they are working or operating. At election time, we might hear that a candidate is running for an office. (Give local example.) That means that they are trying to get a job helping citizens. So, *run* has many different meanings.

run

find

three

from

skip

odd

- Point to the letter that makes each sound as I say it: /r/, /u/, /n/. This word has three letters and three sounds.
- Put *run* back and find the word *find*.
- Find means to locate. Did you *find* the word I asked you to get?
- Show me the letters that make these sounds: /f/, /ī/, /n/, /d/. Now say the word together: *find*. Take off the /f/ sound and say what's left of the word: / īnd/. What are some words that rhyme with *find*? *bind, kind, mind, rind, wind*. These are all spelled the same way, with *i-n-d* at the end.
- Put your finger over the last letter of the word. Now we have the word *fin*. Fish have fins that help them move through the water.
- Put your finger on the first and last letters. Now we have the word *in*. Put *find* back and get the word *three*.
- Let's count off around the room—one, two, three. Every person who is the number three gets to stand up and hold your word for the class to see. (Have kids count off quickly—1, 2, 3, starting over again and continuing around the room, allowing each third child to stand and hold up the word.)
- Put your finger under the first 3 letters that represent the /thr/ sound. This is the same sound as in the words *throw, through,* and *thrift*. These three letters work together.

- Put your finger under the 2 *e*'s. They represent the sound of their own name, *e*, which we call the long-*e* sound.
- Put *three* away and get the word *from*. The beginning *f* has a partner that goes with it to represent the sound /fr/ as in the words *French fry, frost, free,* and *frame*.
- We might use the word *from* in the sentence: *The letter was from Aunt Teresa.*
- Put your finger under the letter that makes the /m/ sound, the *m*.
- Put *from* away and get the word *skip*.
- *Skip* has several different meanings. You might skip on the playground. Can one of you skip across this room to show us?
- *Skip* also means to leave out something. I might call all of your names to line up and accidentally skip a name.
- Put your fingers under the first 2 letters that blend to make the sound /sk/. This is the sound in the beginning of *skate, ski, sky*.
- Show me the vowel that makes the /i/ sound—the short-*i* sound.
- Put your finger under the letter making the /p/ sound, the letter p.
- The pattern for this word, /ip/, will help us spell other words like *lip, sip, rip, nip,* and *tip*. Put *skip* back and get the word *odd*.
- Here's another word that has several meanings. We might consider that something that is different from most other things is *odd*. Odd is not necessarily bad. Odd may be creative or unusual. In math, some numbers are said to be odd and some are even.
- Put your fingers under the last two letters in the word. *Odd* ends with two d's in a row, which is a little unusual, or odd itself!
- Let's collect our new words and save them to use later in the week.

Day 2: Word Whittle

Distribute the Lesson 19 words and have students place them across the top of their work space. Work through the following sets of clues as described on page 32.

First Word:
1. a word that starts with a consonant (*run, find, three, from, skip*)
2. a word that has the letter *r* in it (*run, from, three*)
3. a word that names a number (*three*)

Second Word:
1. a word that has at least 2 tall letters in it (*find, three, odd*)
2. a word that has 2 tall letters side-by-side (*three, odd*)
3. a word that has 2 of the same tall letter (*odd*)

Third Word:
1. a word that is a verb—something you can do (*run, find, skip*)

2. a word that has the vowel *i* in it (*find, skip*)
3. a word that rhymes with *ship* (*skip*)

Fourth Word:

1. a word that has an *i* or an *o* in it (*find, from, skip, odd*)
2. a word that has an *f* in it (*find, from*)
3. a word with a pattern that can help us spell *mind* (*find*)

Day 3: Free Choice Activity Day

Choose one or two of these activities (see pages 18–20):

☐ Word Match ☐ Word Pop ☐ Word Swat
☐ Word Sort ☐ Voice Choice ☐ Cheer the Words
☐ Word Detective ☐ Rhymer ☐ Other: _____

Word Sort

If you choose Word Sort, here are categories that fit this week's words:

- words with 3 or 4 letters
- words with 1 or 2 vowels
- words with tall letters
- words with blended beginnings
- words with long vowel sounds
- words that end with /d/

Day 4: Word Builder

Distribute the letter strip of the Lesson 19 Word Card to each student. Have students separate the letters, reviewing the letter names as they place them in alphabetical order: *a, d, e, g, i, n,* and *r*.

Have students spell words as you call them out. Write each word on the board as students work and offer a sentence to help them understand its meaning. Call out words in this increasingly difficult order, including the shaded words if your students are ready:

in	dare	ran	*red*
ding	age	*range*	*read*
ring	rage	*danger*	*reading*
rang	rag	*grade*	
are	nag	*garden*	

On the board or in a pocket chart, sort the written words according to spelling patterns shown below.

-ing	-age	-ag
ring	age	rag
ding	rage	nag

After you've sorted the words, have students read over the words in each column.

Focus on the *-ing* words. Tell students that if they know this pattern, it can help them spell many other words. Invite students to brainstorm a list of other words that rhyme with ring, recording them on the board: *bing, ding, king, ping, sing, wing, thing, cling, bring, string.*

You may repeat this process with the other spelling patterns as appropriate for your particular students.

Day 5: Word Smart

Distribute the Lesson 19 words, and ask students to arrange them across the top of their desks, leaving work space below.

Ask students to respond to your questions by picking up the correct word(s) and holding it so that you can see their answers.

Can you find . . .

- a word that rhymes with *me*?
- a word that rhymes with *sip*?
- a word that starts with the sound /fr/?
- a word with a pattern that helps us spell *fun*?
- a word with two of the same letter?
- a word that starts the same way as the word *sky*?
- a word hiding the little word *in*?
- a word that starts with a vowel?
- a word that starts with 3 consonants?
- a word that ends with the /p/ sound?
- a word that means "to locate or get?"
- a word that names an activity you might do on the playground?
- a word that starts with the letter *r*?
- a word that ends with the /m/ sound?
- a word that has 2 tall letters together?
- a word with a long-*i* sound?
- a word that fits this sentence: "I got a letter _____ my friend"?

✳ Homework ✳

Send the letters and words home with each student. Parents can use the words as flash cards and the letters to practice making words, as described in the Parent-Child Word Work sheet.

Day 1: Meet the Words

Pass out the Lesson 20 Word Cards, prepared as described on pages 14–15. Have students break apart the 6 new words and spread them on their desks. Ask students to do the following:

- ~~Hold up each card as you pronounce the word on it.~~
- ~~Look at the word, read it aloud, and spell it with you.~~
- ~~Return the word card to the top of their desk.~~

Then guide students through the following activities, saying:

- Put the word *but* in your work space.
- Point to the letter that represents each sound as I say it: /b/, /u/, /t/.

  but

  with

  this

  has

  again

  future

  - (You might as well address what they're thinking!) This *but* is spelled differently from the word that we use for our bottoms. The word that we use for our bottoms is spelled with 2 *t*'s—*butt*.
  - What words rhyme with *but*? (*mut, nut, cut, hut, gut, jut, rut*) Put *but* back and get the word *with*.
  - Put your finger under the letters that represent these sounds: /w/, /i/.
  - Now put your finger under the 2 letters that blend together to represent the sound /th/. So often we see these letter buddies *with* each other, don't we?
  - Answer these questions about *with*: What goes with hotdogs? What goes with vanilla ice cream? Let's put *with* back and get the word *this*.

- Point to the 2 letters at the beginning that make the /th/ sound. There are our letter buddies again! Cover those letter buddies with your finger and see what word we find hiding in this. Yes, *is*!
- I'm going to use *this* is several sentences. I want you to fill in the blank with the object I point to. "This is a _____." (Point to objects in the room. Stress the word *this* and allow students to fill in the blank orally.) Put *this* back and get the word *has*.
- Point to the letter making the sound /h/. Cover up the first 2 letters and let's see what word we have hiding here. It's *as*!
- Let's put the two together: /h/ + *as* = *has*.
- *Has* is part of the *have* family. We might say, "I have a pencil, and you have a pencil." But, we would say, "He has a pencil, and she has a pencil." Sometimes our ears will help us know when

have and *has* are correct. I would never say, "I has a pencil." That wouldn't be correct. Put *has* back and get the word *again*.

- *Again* means "once more." If I say, "Will you tell me your name again?" it means that you've already told me once.
- Point to the first letter, which is the vowel *a*.
- Point to the last letter, which represents the /n/ sound.
- Turn to a buddy and tell them something you would like to do again and again.
- Put *again* back and get the word *future*.
- Sometimes we talk about the past—something that has already happened. Sometimes we talk about the present—what's happening to us now. Sometimes we predict or guess what will happen in the future—what hasn't happened yet.
- Let me ask you what you'd like to be in the future, when you grow up. (Ask students to respond to the question as you restate it each time, emphasizing the word *future*.)
- This word has 2 syllables. Let's clap them as we say them—*fu–ture*.
- Lets trace this word. It has two tall letters, *f* and *t*.
- Studying hard will help you be a great citizen in the future!
- Let's collect our new words and save them to use later in the week.

Day 2: Word Whittle

Distribute the Lesson 20 words and have students place them across the top of their work space. Work through the following sets of clues as described on page 32.

First Word:
4. a word that has one syllable (*but, with, this, has*)
5. a word that has the letter *t* and *h* together (*with, this*)
6. a word that puts things and people together (*with*)

Second Word:
1. a word that has 2 tall letters (*but, with, this, future*)
2. a word that has a *u* in it (*but, future*)
3. a word that means something that hasn't yet happened (*future*)

Third Word:
1. a word that has more than 3 letters (*with, this, again, future*)
2. a word that has 2 syllables (*again, future*)
3. a word that starts with a vowel (*again*)

Fourth Word:
1. a word that starts with a tall letter (*but, this, has, future*)
2. a word that ends with the letter *s* (*this, has*)
3. a word that fits in this sentence: My dog _____ new puppies. (*has*)

Day 3: Free Choice Activity Day

Choose one or two of these activities (see pages 18–20):

☐ Word Match   ☐ Word Pop   ☐ Word Swat

☐ Word Sort   ☐ Voice Choice   ☐ Cheer the Words

☐ Word Detective   ☐ Rhymer   ☐ Other: _____

Word Sort

If you choose Word Sort, here are categories that fit this week's words:

- words with 3 or 4 letters
- words with 1 or 2 vowels
- words with tall letters
- words with short-*i* sound
- words that end with the letter *s*
- words with 2 syllables

Day 4: Word Builder

Distribute the letter strip of the Lesson 20 Word Card to each student. Have students separate the letters, reviewing the letter names as they place them in alphabetical order: *a, d, h, r, s, t, u,* and *y.*

Have students spell words as you call them out. Write each word on the board as students work and offer a sentence to help them understand its meaning. Call out words in this increasingly difficult order, including the shaded words if your students are ready:

at	dry	say	dusty
hat	try	stay	rust
sat	day	stray	rusty
rat	hay	tray	Thursday*
shy	ray	dust	

* *Be sure to point out that days of the week are always capitalized; have students turn over the paper with the* t *on it and write a capital* T *on the back.*

On the board or in a pocket chart, sort the written words according to the following spelling patterns, including -*ust* if your students are ready.

-at	-ay	-ust
sat	day	dust
hat	ray	rust
rat	hay	
	say	
	stay	
	stray	
	tray	

After you've sorted the words, have students read over the words in each column.

Focus on the -*at* words. Tell students that if they know this pattern, it can help them spell many other words. Invite students to brainstorm a list of other words that rhyme with *at*, recording them on the board: *cat, fat, hat, mat, pat, rat, sat, vat, brat, chat, flat, gnat, slat.*

You may repeat this process with the other spelling patterns.

Day 5: Word Smart

Distribute the Lesson 20 words, and ask students to arrange them across the top of their desks, leaving work space below.

Ask students to respond to your questions by picking up the correct word(s) and holding it so that you can see their answers. *Can you find . . .*

- a word that rhymes with *gut?*
- a word that fits in this sentence: "I asked him how to get to his house, but I need to ask him _____"?
- a word with the letter *t* and *h?*
- a word with 2 syllables?
- a word hiding the little word *his?*
- a word hiding the little word *it?*
- a word hiding the little word *as?*
- a word hiding the little word *is?*
- a word ending with the /t/ sound?
- a word ending with the /s/ sound?
- a word that fits in this sentence: "Can you help me carry __ tray?"
- a word that means something hasn't happened yet?
- a word starting with the /w/ sound?
- a word starting with the first letter of the alphabet?
- a word starting with the second letter of the alphabet?
- a word that fits in this sentence: "I hope everyone _____ a good day today!"?

✳ Homework ✳

Send the letters and words home with each student. Parents can use the words as flash cards and the letters to practice making words, as described in the Parent-Child Word Work sheet.

Day 1: Meet the Words

Pass out the Lesson 21 Word Cards, prepared as described on pages 14–15. Have students break apart the 6 new words and spread them on their desks. Ask students to do the following:

- Hold up each card as you pronounce the word on it.
- Look at the word, read it aloud, and spell it with you.
- Return the word card to the top of their desk.

Then guide students through the following activities, saying:

- Put the word will in your workspace. Point to each letter as I make its sound: /w/, /i/, /l/.

will

did

so

no

election

vote

  - Put your finger over the first letter. Now we have the word *ill*. When we are sick, we are ill. This pattern helps us spell words like *bill, chill, dill, pill,* and *grill*.
  - Put the word *did* in your work space.
  - This is a verb that is related to *do* and *done*. We might say, "He did his homework." It tells us that something happened in the past.
  - Point to each of the letters as I make the sounds in this word: /d/, /i/, /d/.
  - Turn to a buddy and tell something you did yesterday. Put *did* back and get the word *so*.
  - This word starts with a snake sound–/s/.
  - The *o* says its own name. This is the long-*o* sound–/ō/.

- I might use it in a sentence like, "We wanted to see the movie, so we went to the theater."
- Can you think of another word that sounds the same but has a different meaning? (Guide students to name *sew* and define it.) Remember, words that sound alike but have different meanings and are spelled differently are called homophones.
- Get the word *no* and put it below *so*. These words have the same spelling pattern and sound pattern–*so, no*.
- Something funny happens, though, when we put *do* alongside these words. *D-o* doesn't have the same sound pattern–*so, no, do*. That's a little tricky, isn't it? Put *so* back and look at *no*.
- *No* means the opposite of *yes*. There is another word pronounced the same way but spelled differently with a different meaning. *K-n-o-w* (write on board) means "to think or be familiar with something." *I know how to get to the library. I know your name.*
- Point to the letter making the /n/ sound in *no*. Point to the letter making the long-*o* sound /ō/. Let's put *no* back and get *election* and *vote*.

- These words are related in their meanings. An election is when people are given a choice about something. When they make their choice, they do it with a vote. Their vote or choice is counted. Whatever choice gets the most votes wins the election. We have elections to choose our mayor, our council members, our governor, our president, and many other offices.
- Let's have an election now! That means everyone gets to make a choice, and everyone's choice or vote is counted. Let's have an election to choose a pet to be the mascot for our classroom (or, choose something else to hold your election about). The mascot will represent us and should tell something about us. (Here you might allude to your local or state sports team's mascot.)
- First we need to make some nominations. That means some of you need to tell us what you would like our mascot to be. (Record those nominations on the board.)
- Next, let's let the people who nominated these mascots tell us why they think they should represent our class.
- Now, in our election, we'll take a vote on which of these will be our mascot. (You can either have a display of hands or a secret ballot if you want to share how real elections allow privacy.)
- In our election, we decided on a mascot for our classroom. Your vote helped determine the mascot. The one with the most votes wins. Our winner is _____!
- Votes and elections are a part of our type of government in a democracy like the United States where we all live. Not all countries allow their citizens to vote. We are lucky that our vote counts!
- Let's collect our new words and save them to use later in the week.

Day 2: Word Whittle

Distribute the Lesson 21 words and have students place them across the top of their work space. Work through the following sets of clues as described on page 32.

First Word:
1. a word that has the vowel *o* in it (*so, no, vote, election*)
2. a word that has a long-*o* sound in it (*so, no, vote*)
3. a word that means the opposite of *yes* (*no*)

Second Word:
1. a word that has 1 syllable (*did, so, will, no, vote*)
2. a word that has at least 1 tall letter (*did, will, vote*)
3. a word that rhymes with *chill* (*will*)

Third Word:
1. a word that has at least 1 tall letter (*did, will, vote, election*)
2. a word that has an *i* in it (*did, will, election*)
3. a word that has 3 syllables (*election*)

Fourth Word:

1. a word that has 1 syllable (*so, no, vote*)
2. a word with only one vowel (*so, no*)
3. a word that begins with the same sound as the word *seven* (*so*)

Day 3: Free Choice Activity Day

Choose one or two of these activities (see pages 18–20):

☐ Word Match   ☐ Word Pop   ☐ Word Swat
☐ Word Sort   ☐ Voice Choice   ☐ Cheer the Words
☐ Word Detective   ☐ Rhymer   ☐ Other: _____

Word Sort

If you choose Word Sort, here are categories that fit this week's words:

- words that sound alike or rhyme
- words that have 1 syllable
- words that have long-*o* sound
- words that have the letter *l*
- words that have the letter *e*
- words that relate to choosing new officials, such as presidents, mayors, governors

Day 4: Word Builder

Distribute the letter strip of the Lesson 21 Word Card to each student. Have students separate the letters, reviewing the letter names as they place them in alphabetical order: *c, e, e, i, l, n, o, s,* and *t*.

Have students spell words as you call them out. Write each word on the board as students work and offer a sentence to help them understand its meaning. Call out words in this increasingly difficult order, including the shaded words if desired:

lie	ice	lone	*elect*
tie	lice	tone	*election*
let	nice	stone	*elections*
net	slice		
set	cone		

On the board or in a pocket chart, sort the written words according to spelling patterns shown below.

-ie	-et	-ice	-one
lie	let	ice	cone
tie	net	lice	lone
	set	nice	tone
		slice	stone

After you've sorted the words, have students read over the words in each column.

Focus on the -*ice* words. Tell students that if they know this pattern, it can help them spell many other words. Invite students to brainstorm a list of other words that rhyme with *ice*, recording them on the board: *dice, lice, mice, nice, rice, vice, price, slice, spice, twice.*

You may repeat this process with the other spelling patterns.

Day 5: Word Smart

Distribute the Lesson 21 words, and ask students to arrange them across the top of their desks, leaving work space below.

Ask students to respond to your questions by picking up the correct word(s) and holding it so that you can see their answers.

Can you find . . .

- a word that rhymes with *frill*?
- a word that rhymes with *tote*?
- a word that rhymes with *hid*?
- a word that rhymes with *spill*?
- a word that rhymes with *toe*?
- a word with 3 syllables?
- a word that has 4 vowels?
- a word with long-*o* sound?
- a word with long-*e* sound?
- a word that means the opposite of *yes*?
- a word that means "to make a choice?"
- a word hiding the word *elect*?
- a word that has 2 of the same letter?
- a word that starts with /d/? ends with /l/?
- a word that starts with a sound a snake might make?
- a word that starts with the same sound as the word *Valentine*?
- a word that ends with the same sound as the word *slid*?

✳ Homework ✳

Send the letters and words home with each student. Parents can use the words as flash cards and the letters to practice making words, as described in the Parent-Child Word Work sheet.

Day 1: Meet the Words

Pass out the Lesson 22 Word Cards, prepared as described on pages 14–15. Have students break apart the 6 new words and spread them on their desks. Ask students to do the following:

- Hold up each card as you pronounce the word on it.
- Look at the word, read it aloud, and spell it with you.
- Return the word card to the top of their desk.

Then guide students through the following activities, saying:

- Put the word *like* in your work space.
- I like chocolate ice cream. Turn to a buddy nearby and tell them something you like.

like

yes

four

me

fly

weather

- Point the letters that make these sounds as I say them: /l/, /ī/, /k/.
- Point to the *e* at the end; it does not represent a sound in this word. We call it a silent *e*.
- *Like* has a pattern that helps us write lots of other words, such as *hike, Mike,* and *bike.*
- Put *like* back and get the word *yes.*
- This word is the opposite of *no.* Answer these questions using yes or no: Do you think it will rain today? Will we have pizza for lunch today?
- Put your finger on the letter making the /y/ sound. The /e/ sound. The /s/ sound.
- Put the word *yes* back and get *four.*

- Fill in the blanks as I say this sentence: *Four* comes after the number _____ and before the number _____.
- Put your finger on the letter that makes the /f/ sound.
- Cover the letter *f* with your finger. Now we have the word *our.* "This is our class with all of our friends and our teacher."
- We've studied another word that sounds like this one. It's the word *f-o-r.* (Write it.) This word is not a number. It is used in sentences like, "Are you ready for lunch?"
- Let's look at this sentence: (Write it.) "I have _____ cookies for lunch." If I have four cookies, how do I write the word? *F-o-u-r.*
- Put *four* back and get the word *me.*
- Let me ask some questions. Stand up with your word *me* and say it if it answers the question: Who is in first grade? Who is a boy? Who is a girl? Who has a dog for a pet? Who loves books? Who likes hotdogs? Good job!

- Point to the letter that makes the /m/ sound.
- Point to the letter that makes the long-e sound. Sometimes there are 2 e's at the end of words that make the long-e sound, but this one only takes 1 *e* to do the job!
- What words rhyme with the word *me*? (*see, bee, be, he, she*)
- Now put *me* back and get the word *fly.*
- Put your fingers under the first 2 letters. These letters blend together to make the sound /fl/. Let's make that sound together, /fl/. The words *flake, flower, flamingo,* and *flight* all start with that sound.
- Point to the last letter, *y*, which represents the long-*i* sound. Because every word has a vowel, the *y* acts as a vowel in this word. *Fly* has several different meanings. A fly is a small insect that we are familiar with.
- We also use the word *fly* to show action. Planes fly, birds fly, and sometimes we say time flies, which means it passes very quickly. Let's all get up, spread our wings (arms), and pretend to fly in place. (Play act this action.)
- Put *fly* back and get the word *weather.*
- Every day we talk about this word. By *weather* we mean the conditions outside—*cold, hot, rainy, sunny, snowy,* and *humid* are some words we use to describe the weather. Turn to a buddy and describe today's weather.
- *Weather* has 2 syllables. Let's clap them as we say them. (Clap *wea-ther.*)
- Let's collect our new words and save them to use later in the week.

Day 2: Word Whittle

Distribute the Lesson 22 words and have students place them across the top of their work space. Work through the following sets of clues as described on page 32.

First Word:
1. a word that has at least 2 vowels (*like, four, weather*)
2. a word that has 2 tall letters (*like, weather*)
3. a word that has 3 vowels in it (*weather*)

Second Word:
1. a word that has fewer than 5 letters (*like, yes, four, me, fly*)
2. a word that has 1 syllable (*yes, fly*)
3. a word that means the opposite of *no* (*yes*)

Third Word:
1. a word that has starts with a tall letter (*like, four, fly*)

2. a word that has a long-*i* sound (*like, fly*)
3. a word that describes what something with wings can do (*fly*)

Fourth Word:

1. a word that has at least 2 vowels (*like, four, weather*)
2. a word that has 2 vowels together (*four, weather*)
3. a word that names a number (*four*)

Day 3: Free Choice Activity Day

Choose one or two of these activities (see pages 18–20):

☐ Word Match   ☐ Word Pop   ☐ Word Swat

☐ Word Sort   ☐ Voice Choice   ☐ Cheer the Words

☐ Word Detective   ☐ Rhymer   ☐ Other: _____

Word Sort

If you choose Word Sort, here are categories that fit this week's words:

- words with 2, 3, or 4 letters
- words with 1, 2, or 3 vowels
- words with tall letters
- words with the long-*i* sound
- words with 1 syllable

Day 4: Word Builder

Distribute the letter strip of the Lesson 22 Word Card to each student. Have students separate the letters, reviewing the letter names as they place them in alphabetical order: *a, a, e, e, h, m, n, r, t,* and *w.*

Have students spell words as you call them out. Write each word on the board as students work and offer a sentence to help them understand its meaning. Call out words in this increasingly difficult order, including the shaded words if your students are ready:

an	met	when	eat	math
ran	net	art	ate	earth
tan	wet	mart	name	weather
man	where	tart	tame	weatherman

On the board or in a pocket chart, sort the written words according to the spelling patterns shown below.

-an	-et	-art	-ame
ran	met	mart	name
tan	net	tart	tame
man	wet		

After you've sorted the words, have students read over the words in each column.

Focus on the -*et* words. Tell students that if they know this pattern, it can help them spell many other words. Invite students to brainstorm a list of other words that rhyme with *met*, recording them on the board: *bet, get, jet, let, net, set, vet, wet.*

You may repeat this process with the other spelling patterns.

You may also want to use this opportunity to teach 3 question words (*what, when, where*) that are used in all content areas. Other features to note include *eat* and *ate* being verbs that are related and that *weatherman* is a compound word.

Day 5: Word Smart

Distribute the Lesson 22 words, and ask students to arrange them across the top of their desks, leaving work space below.

Ask students to respond to your questions by picking up the correct word(s) and holding it so that you can see their answers. *Can you find . . .*

- a word that rhymes with *my*?
- a word that rhymes with *bike*?
- a word that rhymes with *mess*?
- a word that rhymes with *door*?
- a word that is the opposite of *no*?
- a word that comes after *three*?
- a word that has *our* hiding inside?
- a word that has *her* hiding inside?
- a word that starts with /fl/?
- a word that names an insect?
- a word that comes before *five*?
- a word that has 2 different meanings and both fit in the sentence "A ____ can ____ around the room"?
- a word that tells what it's like outside?
- a word that has 3 vowels? that has 2 syllables?
- a word that starts with the /y/ sound?
- a word that has a silent letter at the end?

❋ Homework ❋

Send the letters and words home with each student. Parents can use the words as flash cards and the letters to practice making words, as described in the Parent-Child Word Work sheet.

Day 1: Meet the Words

Pass out the Lesson 23 Word Cards, prepared as described on pages 14–15. Have students break apart the 6 new words and spread them on their desks. Ask students to do the following:

- Hold up each card as you pronounce the word on it.
- Look at the word, read it aloud, and spell it with you.
- Return the word card to the top of their desk.

Then guide students through the following activities, saying:

- Put the word *now* in your work space.
- *Now* is a time word. It means something is taking place right this minute: "Open your book now."

  - Point to the letter that makes the sound /n/.
  - The *o-w* blend together to represent /ou/. That sounds like someone is hurt, doesn't it?
  - The *-ow* pattern will help us read and write many words. If we can spell *now*, we can spell words like *cow, wow, chow, bow,* and *vow.*
  - Get the word *new* and put it just below *now.*
  - How many letters do these words have alike? How many letters are different?
  - When I say the word, point to it. These two words look very much alike. You'll have to listen carefully to choose the right one. (Pronounce each of the 2 words twice so that students have a chance to distinguish between them.)

now

new

to

ran

past

present

- Put *now* back and keep *new* in your work space.
- *New* is the opposite of *old.* We might say, "I have a new book that I want to read." "We have a new student starting in our class today." Let's put *new* back and get the word *to.*
- We've studied another word that sounds like this. (Write *to* and *too* on the board.) This word with double *o*'s means "also." We would use it if we said, "If you go, I will go, too." Any time you can replace the two with also, it's spelled t-o-o.
- Today's *to*, t-o, is used in sentences like "I am going to school today" and "I am going to visit my grandparents."
- There are only 2 sounds in this word. Point to the first letter that makes the /t/ sound. Put your finger under the second letter that represents the /o͞o/ sound.
- Put *to* back and get the word *ran.*

- *Ran* is a verb, an action word. "John ran as fast as he could."
- Point to the letters that make these sounds: /r/, /a/, /n/.
- Cover the *r* with your finger. The *-an* pattern will help us read and spell other words. If we can spell *ran*, we can spell words like *ban, can, Dan, fan, tan,* and *man.* Put *ran* back and get *past.*
- In social studies, we'll talk about things that happened in the past. It is a time word. If something happened in the past, it happened before now. The past could be yesterday, or the past could be hundreds of years ago.
- Point to the letters that make these sounds: /p/, /a/. Point to the *s* and *t* that blend together to make the sound /st/. *S* and *t* are buddies in the sound they make together in words.
- Put *past* back and get *present.* Point to the letter that you think makes the /z/ sound. Notice that it's an *s* that sounds like a *z.*
- *Present* has 2 syllables. Clap with me: *pre-sent.*
- This is another time word. The present is what is happening now. In the present, we are studying words. Three weeks ago we had the word *future.* That's what hasn't yet happened. So, we have *past, present* and *future* as words to refer to time.
- Tell me whether this person is a president from the past, or in the present, or the future: Abraham Lincoln, Barack Obama (or current president), you!
- Now, *present* also has a completely different meaning. A present can be something we all love to receive. A present can be a gift. If you could have any present you want, tell a buddy right now what you would like for it to be.
- So *present* can be a gift or it can be a time word.
- Let's collect our new words and save them to use later in the week.

Day 2: Word Whittle

Distribute the Lesson 23 words and have students place them across the top of their work space. Work through the following sets of clues as described on page 32.

First Word:
1. a word that has an *n* in it (*now, ran, new*)
2. a word that starts with the /n/ sound (*now, new*)
3. a word that rhymes with *cow* (*now*)

Second Word:
1. a word that has a tall letter in it (*too, past, present*)
2. a word that has 2 of the same letter in it (*too, present*)
3. a word that 2 syllables (*present*)

Third Word:

1. a word that refers to time (*now, past, present*)
2. a word that ends with the /t/ sound (*past, present*)
3. a word that rhymes with *fast* (*past*)

Fourth Word:

1. a word that has 3 letters (*now, too, ran, new*)
2. words that share 2 of the same letters (*now, new*)
3. a word that means the opposite of *old* (*new*)

Day 3: Free Choice Activity Day

Choose one or two of these activities (see pages 18–20):

- ☐ Word Match   ☐ Word Pop   ☐ Word Swat
- ☐ Word Sort   ☐ Voice Choice ☐ Cheer the Words
- ☐ Word Detective ☐ Rhymer   ☐ Other: _____

Word Sort

If you choose Word Sort, here are categories that fit this week's words:

- words with 3 letters
- words with 1 or 2 vowels
- words with tall letters
- words with letters below the line
- words with the short-*a* sound
- words with 1 syllable
- time words

Day 4: Word Builder

Distribute the letter strip of the Lesson 23 Word Card to each student. Have students separate the letters, reviewing the letter names as they place them in alphabetical order: *a, a, d, r, s, t, u,* and *y.*

Have students spell words as you call them out. Write each word on the board as students work and offer a sentence to help them understand its meaning. Call out words in this increasingly difficult order, including the shaded words if your students are ready:

at	art	say	try	rusty
sat	dart	ray	rust	dusty
rat	day	dry	dust	Saturday*

* Have students turn over the s card and write a capital S on the back. Discuss how we capitalize the days of the week.

On the board or in a pocket chart, sort the written words

according to spelling patterns below, including the shaded ones if desired:

-at	-ay	-y	-ust	-usty
sat	day	try	rust	rusty
rat	say	dry	dust	dusty
	ray			

After you've sorted the words, have students read over the words in each column.

Focus on the -*y* words. Tell students that if they know this pattern, it can help them spell many other words. Invite students to brainstorm a list of other words that rhyme with *dry*, recording them on the board: *cry, my, ply, pry, spy, sly, sty, try.*

If students suggest other words that end with the long-*i* sound, discuss that several letter combinations can represent that sound and sort the words they suggest. For instance, *pie, die; sigh, high; buy; dye, bye.* You may repeat this process with the other spelling patterns as appropriate for your particular students.

Day 5: Word Smart

Distribute the Lesson 23 words, and ask students to arrange them across the top of their desks, leaving work space below.

Ask students to respond to your questions by picking up the correct word(s) and holding it so that you can see their answers. *Can you find . . .*

- a word that rhymes with *tan? goo? fan? shoe? fast?*
- a word that can mean "a gift"? is the opposite of *old?*
- a word that ends with the /t/ sound?
- a word that starts with the /r/ sound? /n/ sound?
- a word that sounds like a number but isn't one?
- a word that means something is happening now?
- a word that means something has already happened?
- a word with the sound /ou/? has 2 syllables?
- a word that fits in this sentence: "I am going ___ school"?
- a word that fits this sentence: "George Washington was a _____ president"?
- two words that are spelled the same except for 1 letter?

✳ Homework ✳

Send the letters and words home with each student. Parents can use the words as flash cards and the letters to practice making words, as described in the Parent-Child Word Work sheet.

Day 1: Meet the Words

Pass out the Lesson 24 Word Cards, prepared as described on pages 14–15. Have students break apart the 6 new words and spread them on their desks. Ask students to do the following:

- Hold up each card as you pronounce the word on it.
- Look at the word, read it aloud, and spell it with you.
- Return the word card to the top of their desk.

Then guide students through the following activities, saying:

- Put the word *eat* in your work space.
- Two letters together represent the long-*e* sound /ē/. Point to those 2 letters. Sometimes, "when 2 vowels go walking, the first one does the talking"!

eat

ate

him

could

heat

freezing

- Point to the letter making the /t/ sound.
- We have to eat to live. Our bodies need food for nourishment. What are some foods that we can eat to stay healthy?
- *Eat* is a verb, an action word. Put the word *ate* right below the word *eat*. Notice that both words have the same letters, but they are in different places. If we want to talk about eating that happened in the past, we use *ate*, which is the form of *eat* that shows the action happened in the past. I *ate* breakfast this morning. I will *eat* lunch soon.
- Put *eat* back with the other words, and let's look at *ate*. Point to the first letter that makes the long-*a* sound. It says its own letter name: *a*.
- Point to the letter making the sound /t/. Notice that the last letter, *e*, is silent. This word has three letters but only two sounds.
- Put your finger over the silent letter, and you'll see the little word *at* hiding there. Without the silent *e*, the *a* now represents the short-*a* sound, /a/.
- This whole word, *a-t-e*, is a pattern in some words. If we added a *g* to the word, it would become *gate*. Tell me what word we would have if we added a *d*? an *h*? an *m*?
- Put *ate* back and get the word *him*.
- *Him* refers to a boy or man. We might say, "Do you want him to go with you?" "Let's play with him on the playground."
- Point to the letters that make these sounds: /h/, /i/, /m/. This word has three sounds and three letters. Put *him* back and get *could*.
- *Could* is a verb that tells that something possibly can be done. "We could go to the park if it doesn't rain."
- Point to the first letter, which represents the /k/ sound.
- This word is very tricky with its spelling because we don't hear the

sounds of all of these letters. When I say the word slowly, listen to see if you can hear an *l*. (Say word slowly.)

- Because of its tricky spelling, we'll just have to remember how it's spelled. Let's point to the letter and say the letter names together–*c-o-u-l-d*. (Repeat.) Let's trace the word with our fingers. It has two tall letters at the end. Let's spell it again: *c-o-u-l-d*.
- Put *could* back and get the words *heat* and *eat*.
- These words both have the same spelling patterns, and they rhyme. Let's say them: *heat, eat*.
- Now you know that if we use the *e-a-t* spelling pattern and add an *h*, it spells *heat*. What if we put an *s* at the beginning of *eat*? What if we put an *m*? An *n*? This is a helpful spelling pattern.
- Put *eat* back, and let's look more closely at *heat*.
- *Heat* results when tiny molecules move around quickly, causing something to get warmer and warmer. Heat can be a noun or a verb. I can say, "The heat from the oven is making the kitchen too hot." Or, I can say, "Let's heat up the hotdogs and eat them."
- Put *heat* back and get *freezing*. These words are almost opposites in temperature. *Heat* means hot and *freezing* is very cold.
- If heat is made by tiny molecules that we can't see moving at a fast rate, what do you think happens to those same molecules when something is freezing? What do you find in your freezer at home? How do you know when something is frozen?
- Sometimes we use *freeze* in another way–to mean stopping what you're doing. Let's all get up and walk around the room. When I say "freeze" that means to stop exactly the way you are, just as through you have become a block of ice. (Play this game for a short while.)
- Let's look at the word. Put your finger on the first two letters, which blend to say /fr/. Put your finger under the 2 *e*'s. Together they make the long-*e* sound, /ē /.
- Put your finger under the letter that makes the /z/ sound.
- Let's collect our new words and save them to use later in the week.

Day 2: Word Whittle

Distribute the Lesson 24 words and have students place them across the top of their work space. Work through the following sets of clues as described on page 32.

First Word:

1. a word that has a *t* in it (*eat, ate, heat*)
2. a word that starts with a vowel (*eat, ate*)
3. a word that rhymes with another word in our list this week (*eat–heat*)

Second Word:

1. a word that has 1 syllable (*eat, ate, him, could, heat*)

2. a word that starts with the /h/ sound (*him, heat*)
3. a word that fits in this sentence: I will ask _ to come with us. (*him*)

Third Word:

1. a word that has a long-e sound (*eat, heat, freezing*)
2. a word that refers to temperature (*heat, freezing*)
3. a word that has 2 syllables (*freezing*)

Fourth Word:

1. a word that has a tall letter (*eat, ate, him, could, heat, freezing*)
2. a word that with 2 tall letters (*could, heat*)
3. a word that rhymes with *should* (*could*)

Day 3: Free Choice Activity Day

Choose one or two of these activities (see pages 18–20):

- ☐ Word Match ☐ Word Pop ☐ Word Swat
- ☐ Word Sort ☐ Voice Choice ☐ Cheer the Words
- ☐ Word Detective ☐ Rhymer ☐ Other: _____

Word Sort

If you choose Word Sort, here are categories that fit this week's words:

- words with 3 letters
- words with 1, 2, or 3 vowels
- words with tall letters
- words with long vowel sounds
- words with 1 syllable
- temperature words

Day 4: Word Builder

Distribute the letter strip of the Lesson 24 Word Card to each student. Have students separate the letters, reviewing the letter names as they place them in alphabetical order: *a, d, d, e, e, n, s, w,* and *y*.

Have students spell words as you call them out. Write each word on the board as students work and offer a sentence to help them understand its meaning. Call out words in this increasingly difficult order, including the shaded words if your students are ready:

ad	and	weed	sway	swan
dad	sand	day	saw	Wednesday*
sad	need	way	new	
send	seed	say	news	

> ** Have students flip over the w card and write a capital on the back. Remind them that the days of the week always start with a capital letter.*

On the board or in a pocket chart, sort the written words according to spelling patterns shown below, including the three-letter chunks if your students are ready:

-ad	-ay	-end	-and	-eed
dad	day	send	sand	seed
sad	say			weed
	way			need
	sway			

After you've sorted the words, have students read over the words in each column.

Focus on the *-ad* words. Tell students that if they know this pattern, it can help them spell many other words. Invite students to brainstorm a list of other words that rhyme with *dad*, recording them on the board: *bad, had, lad, mad, pad, sad, tad, Brad, glad*. You may want to point out some capitalization rules: If *dad* is used in place of a father's name, it is capitalized. "My dad is a fisherman." "I'm going with Dad to the store." If your dad's name is Steve, you wouldn't say, "My Steve is a fisherman," so you know to keep *dad* lowercase. But, "I'm going with Steve to the store" makes sense, so we know to capitalize *dad* in that case. And names are always capitalized: *Brad*.

Day 5: Word Smart

Distribute the Lesson 24 words, and ask students to arrange them across the top of their desks, leaving work space below.

Ask students to respond to your questions by picking up the correct word(s) and holding it so that you can see their answers. *Can you find . . .*

- a word that is hiding the little word *eat*? *free*?
- a word that rhymes with *mate*? *meat*? *cheat*?
- a word that starts with the /fr/ sound? /h/ sound?
- a word that is a result of tiny molecules moving fast?
- a word that has the long-e sound in it? the word *at* hiding in it?
- a word that ends with the /m/ sound?
- a word that starts with the same sound as *cap*?
- two words that have exactly the same letters in them?
- a word that has 2 syllables? ends with the /t/ sound?.
- a word that sounds like the name of a number but is spelled very differently? (*ate*)
- two words that start with the same sound?

✳ Homework ✳

Send the letters and words home with each student. Parents can use the words as flash cards and the letters to practice making words, as described in the Parent-Child Word Work sheet.

Day 1: Meet the Words

Pass out the Lesson 25 Word Cards, prepared as described on pages 14–15. Have students break apart the 6 new words and spread them on their desks. Ask students to do the following:

- Hold up each card as you pronounce the word on it.
- Look at the word, read it aloud, and spell it with you.
- Return the word card to the top of their desk.

Then guide students through the following activities, saying:

- Put the word *of* in your work space.
- *Of* is what we might call a glue word. It helps to hold sentences and thoughts together. I might say, "We will read a book of poems." Or, "Do you want a glass of water?"

of
much
ask
open
hero
honor

- Point to each letter as I say it: *o, f*. Let's spell *of* together: *o-f*.
- Put *of* back and get the word *much*.
- Point to the first letter that makes the /m/ sound.
- Slide your finger to the next letter that makes the /u/ sound.
- Put your finger under the last two letters. Together they make the /ch/ sound. Words like *crunch, lunch,* and *munch* end with this same pair of letters.
- Sometimes *much* means a measure or amount of something. I might say, "I have too much food on my plate!" Or, "We haven't had much rain."
- Put *much* back and get the word *ask*.
- This word starts with the same sound as *apple*.
- The *s* and *k* are buddies that represent the blended sound /sk/. Let's say /sk/ together. (Repeat it several times with them.) This is the same /sk/ sound in the word *skip*.
- *Ask* usually involves a question. Turn to a buddy and ask them a question.
- Put *ask* away and get the word *open*. *Open* is the opposite of *close*. We open the door, and we close the door. (You might ask a student to demonstrate this with the classroom door.)
- This word starts by saying its own letter name /ō/.
- Now cover the *o* with your finger and you'll see the word *pen*. Pigs live in a pen. Sometimes we write with a pen.
- Put *open* back and get the word *hero*.
- We see many superheroes on TV and in the movies. Can you name some?

- We also have heroes in real life. Heroes are people who do outstanding things to help other people—not to get paid for it, but to help. What real heroes can you think of?
- This word has 2 syllables. Let's clap them—*he-ro*.
- Cover the last 2 letters with your hand. Now we have the word *he*.
- Cover the last letter with your hand, and we now have *her*.
- Some of our heroes are veterans. (Write the word on the board.) They are the people who have served or are now serving in the Army, Navy, Air Force, Marines, or Coast Guard to protect our country. Maybe you have a parent, a grandparent, a relative, or a friend who is a veteran. Some veterans have died to help our country. They truly are heroes!
- Put the word *hero* back and get the word *honor*.
- *Honor* means "a quality of respect, honesty, and fairness." We might say that veterans are people of honor. Also, if we honor someone, we treat them with great respect.
- *Honor* is a tricky word to spell. When we say it, we don't hear the sound of the *h*. It's silent.
- We have 2 little words hiding inside of *honor*. Put your finger on the *o* and *n* that spell *on*.
- Put your finger on the *o* and *r* that spell *or*.
- Let's say the word again together—*honor*.
- Let's collect our new words and save them to use later in the week.

Day 2: Word Whittle

Distribute the Lesson 25 words and have students place them across the top of their work space. Work through the following sets of clues as described on page 32.

First Word:
1. a word with 2 syllables *(hero, honor, open)*
2. a word that has a long-*o* sound *(hero, open)*
3. a word that starts with the /h/ sound *(hero)*

Second Word:
1. a word that has a tall letter *(of, ask, hero, honor, much)*
2. a word that starts with a vowel *(of, ask)*
3. a word that ends with the same sound that *skip* starts with *(ask)*

Third Word:
1. a word with the vowel *o* in it *(hero, honor, open)*
2. a word that starts with an *h* *(hero, honor)*
3. a word that starts with an *h* that is silent *(honor)*

Fourth Word

1. a word that starts with a vowel (*of, ask, open*)
2. a word that has a tall letter (*of, ask*)
3. a word that ends with the letter *f* (*of*)

Day 3: Free Choice Activity Day

Choose one or two of these activities (see pages 18–20):

- ☐ Word Match
- ☐ Word Pop
- ☐ Word Swat
- ☐ Word Sort
- ☐ Voice Choice
- ☐ Cheer the Words
- ☐ Word Detective
- ☐ Rhymer
- ☐ Other: _____

Word Sort

If you choose Word Sort, here are categories that fit this week's words:

- words with 2, 3, 4, or 5 letters
- words with 1 or 2 vowels
- words with tall letters
- words with long vowel sounds
- words with 1 or 2 syllables
- words that start with *h*
- words that start or end with vowels

Day 4: Word Builder

Distribute the letter strip of the Lesson 25 Word Card to each student. Have students separate the letters, reviewing the letter names as they place them in alphabetical order: *a, e, e, n, r, s, t,* and *v.*

Have students spell words as you call them out and write them on the board:

tan	vest	vent	rave
ran	rest	sent	veteran
van	nest	rent	veterans
vans	ear	save	

On the board or in a pocket chart, sort the written words according to the spelling patterns below, including the shaded patterns if desired:

-an	-est	-ent	-ave
tan	vest	vent	rave
van	nest	sent	save
ran	rest	rent	

After you've sorted the words, have students read over the words in each column. Focus on the -*est* words. Tell students that if they know this pattern, it can help them spell many other words. Invite students to brainstorm a list of other words that rhyme with *vest*, recording them on the board: *best, jest, lest, nest, pest, rest, test, west, zest, chest.*

You may also want to do a quick review of forming plurals by adding -*s: van/vans, ear/ears, vent/vents, veteran/veterans*

Day 5: Word Smart

Distribute the Lesson 21 words, and ask students to arrange them across the top of their desks, leaving work space below.

Ask students to respond to your questions by picking up the correct word(s) and holding it so that you can see their answers.

Can you find . . .

- A word that starts with an *o*?
- A word that starts with a silent letter?
- A word that rhymes with *task*?
- A word that is hiding the word *he*?
- A word that is hiding the word *her*?
- A word that is hiding the word *pen*?
- A word that is hiding the word *or*?
- A word that with an *m* added to the beginning would be *mask*?
- A word that means the opposite of *closed*?
- A word that fits in this sentence: "Do you have a question you want to _____?"
- A word that has the long-*o* sound in it?
- A word that ends with the same sound that *chocolate* begins with?
- A word that has the fewest letters of this week's words?
- A word that has the most letters of this week's words?
- A word that fits in this sentence: "How _____ money will I need to buy that game?"
- A word that describes many fire fighters, police officers, and members of the armed forces?
- A word that fits in this sentence: "Are you afraid ____ snakes?"

✳ Homework ✳

Send the letters and words home with each student. Parents can use the words as flash cards and the letters to practice making words, as described in the Parent-Child Word Work sheet.

Day 1: Meet the Words

Pass out the Lesson 26 Word Cards, prepared as described on pages 14–15. Have students break apart the 6 new words and spread them on their desks. Ask students to do the following:

- Hold up each card as you pronounce the word on it.
- Look at the word, read it aloud, and spell it with you.
- Return the word card to the top of their desk.

Then guide students through the following activities, saying:

- Put the word *as* in your work space.
- We use this little word in many ways. We can use it to say, "It's *as* hot today *as* it was yesterday." Or we could say, "There are many types of flowers in our garden, such *as* roses and daisies." Turn to a partner and make up a sentence that uses the word *as*. (Give students a minute, then invite pairs to share sentences.)
- This word has one vowel and one consonant. Let's point to the vowel first, then the consonant.
- What would happen if we added an *h* to the beginning of the word? Yes, the word would be *has*. Put *as* back and get the word *them*.
- We use the word *them* when we're talking about several other people. We might say, "Tell them to come in out of the rain."
- Put your finger under the 2 letters that make the /th/ sound. Point to the letter that represents the /m/ sound.
- Cover the last letter with your finger. What word do we have now?
- Cover the first and last letters with your fingers. Now we have the word *he*. Put *them* back and get the word *many*.
- *Many* refers to the number of something. If we have many apples, we have a lot of them. There are many students in this class!
- Point to the letter that makes the /m/ sound.
- Listen for the last sound in the word: *many*. What is the last sound? Yes, the long-*e* sound, /ē/. In this word, the long-*e* sound is represented by the *y*. Cover the first and last letters with your fingers. What word do you see? Yes, *an*.
- Put *many* back and get the word *would*. This word is tricky, just like the word *could*, which we had two weeks ago. We won't hear the *l* at all. We'll have to remember how this word is spelled.
- Put your finger on the letter that makes the /w/ sound.
- Put your finger on the ending sound /d/.

as

them

many

would

character

setting

- Cover the first letter with your finger. If we put a *c* there, what would the word be? An *s* and *h*?
- I might say, "Would you like to read this book?" Or, "He would like to read the first chapter."
- Put *would* back and get the big word *character*.
- Many times when *ch-* is at the beginning of a word it makes the /ch/ sound. This time it makes a hard-*c* sound /k/.
- This word has 3 syllables. Let's clap them—*char-ac-ter*.
- In our reading, we'll talk about the characters in our stories. They are the people our stories are about. Sometimes animals are characters. (Recall a character in one of the stories you've read.)
- *Character* is also a word we use to describe what someone is like—their qualities or traits. I might say, "Abraham Lincoln was a man of good character. He was even called Honest Abe."
- Put *character* back and get the word *setting*.
- This is another word we use to talk about the stories we read. *Setting* is the time and place in which a story happens. The setting might be in the past, the present, or the future, and it might take place in a town like ours. (Recall a setting in a familiar story.)
- Point to the sounds in this word as I say them slowly—/s/, /e/, t/. Point to the last 3 letters that represent the /ing/ sound.
- The *-ing* pattern will help us spell many words, such as *ring, sing, fling,* and *swimming*.
- This word has 2 syllables. Let's clap them—*set-ting*.
- Let's collect our new words and save them to use later in the week.

Day 2: Word Whittle

Distribute the Lesson 26 words and have students place them across the top of their work space. Work through the following sets of clues as described on page 32.

First Word:
1. a word that has a tall letter (*them, would, character, setting*)
2. a word that has 2 tall letters together (*them, would, setting*)
3. a word that tells when and where a story happens (*setting*)

Second Word:
1. a word that has the vowel *e* in it (*them, character, setting*)
2. a word that doesn't have any letters below the line (*character, them*)
3. a word that is what we call the people or sometimes animals in a story (*character*)

Third Word:

1. a word with more than 3 letters in it (*them, would, character, setting*)
2. a word with 1 syllable (*them, would*)
3. a word that rhymes with *should* (*would*)

Fourth Word:

1. a word that is not the longest or shortest of our words (*them, many, would, setting*)
2. a word that has only 1 vowel (*them, many*)
3. a word that starts with a /th/ sound (*them*)

Day 3: Free Choice Activity Day

Choose one or two of these activities (see pages 18–20):

☐ Word Match ☐ Word Pop ☐ Word Swat

☐ Word Sort ☐ Voice Choice ☐ Cheer the Words

☐ Word Detective ☐ Rhymer ☐ Other: _____

Word Sort

If you choose Word Sort, here are categories that fit this week's words:

- words with 2, 3, 4, or 5 letters
- words with 1 or 2 vowels
- words with tall letters
- words with long vowel sounds
- words with 1 or 2 syllables
- words that start or end with vowels

Day 4: Word Builder

Distribute the letter strip of the Lesson 26 Word Card to each student. Have students separate the letters, reviewing the letter names as they place them in alphabetical order: *a, a, c, c, e, h, r, r, s,* and *t.*

Have students spell words as you call them out and write them on the board:

car	scar	art	character
tar	rest	cart	characters
star	chest	chart	

On the board or in a pocket chart, sort the written words according to spelling patterns shown below.

-ar	-est	-art
car	rest	chart
tar	chest	cart
star		
scar		

After you've sorted the words, have students read over the words in each column. Focus on the *-art* words. Tell students that if they know this pattern, it can help them spell many other words. Invite students to brainstorm a list of other words that rhyme with *art*, recording them on the board: *Bart, cart, dart, hart, mart, part, tart, chart, start.*

If you include *hart*, be sure to point out that it's a different word from *heart*; it means "a male deer." If you include *Bart*, remind students about the importance of capitalizing proper names.

Day 5: Word Smart

Distribute the Lesson 26 words, and ask students to arrange them across the top of their desks, leaving work space below.

Ask students to respond to your questions by picking up the correct word(s) and holding it so that you can see their answers. *Can you find . . .*

- a word that starts with a vowel?
- a word that starts with a /th/ sound?
- a word that rhymes with *Tim? could?*
- a word that is hiding the little word *he?*
- a word that is hiding the word *set?*
- a word that would be *has* if it had an *h* at the beginning?
- a word that sounds the same as the word that means "the material trees are made of?"
- a word that starts with the sound /m/?
- a word with 2 of the same letter in it?
- a word with the /ing/ sound on the end?
- a word that ends with the long-*e* sound?
- a word that ends with an *s?*
- a word that sounds like it starts with a *k*, but it doesn't?
- a word that means "when and where a story happens?"
- a word that refers to who the story is about?
- a word that starts with the /w/ sound? the /a/ sound?
- the word that is the longest in this week's group? the shortest?

* Homework *

Send the letters and words home with each student. Parents can use the words as flash cards and the letters to practice making words, as described in the Parent-Child Word Work sheet.

Day 1: Meet the Words

Pass out the Lesson 27 Word Cards, prepared as described on pages 14–15. Have students break apart the 6 new words and spread them on their desks. Ask students to do the following:

- Hold up each card as you pronounce the word on it.
- Look at the word, read it aloud, and spell it with you.
- Return the word card to the top of their desk.

Then guide students through the following activities, saying:

- Put the word *over* in your work space.
- *Over* has several meanings. Sometimes it means that something has ended, like, "The movie is over." Another meaning of *over* is "above" as in, "The clouds hung over the town all day; then it rained."
  - Point to the first letter that says its own name– the letter that represents the long-*o* sound /ō/.
  - The *e* and *r* are buddies that together make the sound /er/.
  - Let's put *over* back and get the word *any*.
  - *Any* usually refers to one or more of something. I might say to another teacher, "Do you have any students who want to come to our play?"
  - If we put the /m/ sound in front of this word, it becomes *many*, one of our words from last week.
  - Point to the *y* on the end that represents the long-*e* sound, just like it does in *many*.
- Put your finger over the last letter. What word is hiding there?
- This little word has 2 syllables. Let's clap them–*an-y*.
- Put *any* back and get the word *know*.
- *Know* is a tricky word because it starts with a silent letter; the *k* doesn't make a sound.
- It also sounds just like the little word *n-o*. (Write this.) *Know* and *no* are homophones. These 2 words have very different meanings. *N-o* is the opposite of *yes*; *k-n-o-w* means "to understand or be acquainted with something or someone."
- I might say, "I know how to read." Or, "Do you know his name?"
- Put your finger over the first letter. What word do you find? If we remember that *now* is hiding in this word, it will help us spell it correctly when we write.
- Put one finger over the first letter and one over the last. What word is hiding there? We have the other little word that sounds the same as our 4 letter word!

over

any

know

don't

insect

cycle

- Put *know* back and get *don't*.
- This word has a mark in it called an apostrophe, just like the word *can't*, which we studied a few weeks ago.
- Put your finger on the apostrophe. An apostrophe is used to tell us that letters are missing. This word is what we call a contraction. (Write this.) A contraction puts two words together and shortens one of them.
- *Don't* is *do not* put together and shortened. (Write on the board and show how they are joined.) Which letter has been left out? (You may wish to share several other contractions at this time.)
- We use contractions in our everyday speech and in some of the writing we do if we want it to sound the way we talk.
- Put *don't* back and get the word *insect*.
- Insects are bugs that have bodies divided into 3 parts. (Sketch this if you can.) They have 3 pairs of legs and usually have 2 pairs of wings. (Add to your drawing.) Some insects are flies, crickets, mosquitoes, grasshoppers, beetles, butterflies, and bees.
- Turn to a buddy and tell them what insect you've seen recently.
- This word has two syllables. Let's clap them: *in-sect*.
- Put *insect* back and get *cycle*. *Cycle* means "a process that repeats or happens again and again in the same sequence." We study the life cycle of animals and the water cycle in science.
- How many *c*'s do you see in this word? Put your finger on the first one and listen as I tell you how it sounds–/s/.
- Now put your finger on the second one and listen as I make its sound–/k/. This word has both of the sounds that *c* can represent.
- Put your finger on the *y*. It makes the long-*i* sound /ī/.
- Move your finger over each letter as I make its sound.
- Let's collect our new words and save them to use later in the week.

Day 2: Word Whittle

Distribute the Lesson 27 words and have students place them across the top of their work space. Work through the following sets of clues as described on page 32.

First Word:
1. a word that has four or fewer letters (*over, any, know, don't*)
2. a word that has the vowel *o* (*over, know, don't*)
3. a word that has a tall letter (*know, don't*)
4. a word that is a contraction (*don't*)

Second Word:
1. a word that has a tall letter in it (*know, don't, cycle, insect*)
2. a word that starts with a consonant (*know, don't, cycle*)
3. a word that has a *c* in it (*cycle, insect*)

4. a word that means "a process that repeats again and again" (*cycle*)

Third Word:

1. a word that doesn't have a *y* in it (*over, know, don't, insect*)
2. a word with the vowel *o* (*over, know, don't*)
3. a word with a tall letter (*know, don't*)
4. a word with a silent letter at the beginning (*know*)

Fourth Word:

1. a word that is not a contraction (*over, any, know, cycle, insect*)
2. a word that has two syllables (*over, any, cycle, insect*)
3. a word that starts with a vowel (*over, any, insect*)
4. a word that means the opposite of *under* (*over*)

Day 3: Free Choice Activity Day

Choose one or two of these activities (see pages 18–20):

☐ Word Match   ☐ Word Pop   ☐ Word Swat

☐ Word Sort   ☐ Voice Choice   ☐ Cheer the Words

☐ Word Detective   ☐ Rhymer   ☐ Other: _____

Word Sort

If you choose Word Sort, here are categories that fit this week's words:

- words with 3, 4, 5, or 6 letters   • words with tall letters
- words with long vowel sounds   • words with 1 or 2 syllables
- words that start or end with vowels

Day 4: Word Builder

Distribute the letter strip of the Lesson 27 Word Card to each student. Have students separate the letters, reviewing the letter names as they place them in alphabetical order: *a, e, g, h, o, p, p, r, r, s,* and *s.*

Have students spell words as you call them out and write them on the board:

hope	shop	rap	rag
rope	shops	gap	sag
hop	he	sap	grass
	she		grasshopper

On the board or in a pocket chart, sort the written words according to spelling patterns below.

-ope	-op	-e	-ap	-ag
hope	hop	he	rap	rag
rope	shop	she	gap	sag
			sap	

After you've sorted the words, have students read over the words in each column. Focus on the *-ope* words. Tell students that if they know this pattern, it can help them spell many other words. Invite students to brainstorm a list of other words that rhyme with *hope*, recording them on the board: *cope, lope, mope, nope, pope, rope, slope, grope, elope.*

Take the opportunity to talk about pronouns that are used to take the place of names in what we read and write. In this activity, you have *he* and *she;* the letters can also spell *her* and *hers.*

Day 5: Word Smart

Distribute the Lesson 27 words, and ask students to arrange them across the top of their desks, leaving work space below.

Ask students to respond to your questions by picking up the correct word(s) and holding it so that you can see their answers. *Can you find . . .*

- a word that starts with a vowel?
- a word that rhymes with *clover? many? slow?*
- a word that is a contraction?
- a word that means "to understand?"
- a word that is a bug that has 3 sections to its body?
- a word that is hiding the word *no?* the word *in?*
- a word that starts with the sound /d/?
- a word that begins with the same sound as the word *open?*
- a word that ends with the sound /t/?
- a word that means "do not?"
- a word that could be a bee, a grasshopper, or a beetle?
- the word that is the longest on the list? the shortest?
- a word that is hiding the word *now?*
- a word with a *y* that makes a long-*i* sound?
- a word with a *y* that makes a long-*e* sound?
- a word that has an apostrophe in it?
- a word that has 2 syllables?
- a word that starts with a silent letter?
- a word that starts with the first letter of the alphabet?
- a word with a *c* that makes an *s* sound /s/ and a *k* sound /k/?

✳ Homework ✳

Send the letters and words home with each student. Parents can use the words as flash cards and the letters to practice making words, as described in the Parent-Child Word Work sheet.

Day 1: Meet the Words

Pass out the Lesson 28 Word Cards, prepared as described on pages 14–15. Have students break apart the 6 new words and spread them on their desks. Ask students to do the following:

- Hold up each card as you pronounce the word on it.
- Look at the word, read it aloud, and spell it with you.
- Return the word card to the top of their desk.

Then guide students through the following activities, saying:

- Put the word *just* in your work space.
- We might use this word to mean *only*. I might say, "I just want you to go with me."

just

take

may

before

length

half

- *Just* can also mean "fair." I might say, "Staying in at recess was just treatment for what he did."
- Point to the letters making the sounds that I make: /j/, /u/, /s/, /t/.
- This word starts the same way that months January, June, and July start. Does anyone have a birthday in those "J" months?
- Cover the first letter again. If we put an *m* there instead of the *j*, the word would be *must*. What if we put an *r* there?
- Put the word *just* back and get the word *take*.
- Point to the letters in the word as I make their sounds–/t/, /a/, /k/.
- Notice that the *e* is silent, and the *a* represents the long-*a* sound.
- Cover the first letter. If we put an *m* there, we have the word *make*. What word do we have if we put an *s-h* there?
- Put *take* back and get the word *may*.
- There is a month called May, but this can't be the month because all months start with uppercase letters. Does anyone have a May birthday?
- This *may* is a polite word. I might say, "May I help you?" Or, "May I leave the dinner table now?"
- There is a long-*a* sound–*a* says its own letter name. When *a* and *y* are together, they represent the long-*a* sound.
- Put *may* away and get the word *before*.
- *Before* means something that happens ahead of something else. I might say, "You need to brush your teeth before you go to bed." That means you'll brush first and then go to bed.
- Cover the *b-e* with one finger and the last letter *e* with a finger.

Now we have the word *for*. The little word *or* is hiding there, too. Do you see it?

- Put *before* away and get the word *length*.
- Length means how long something is. We can measure something to find out its length. We might use inches, feet, yards, or miles to tell how long something is. (Demonstrate measuring something with a ruler.)
- Even though this is a long word, it has only one syllable. Let's clap it: *length*.
- This word has the *t-h* partners that represent the /th/ sound that is also in *think*, *thunder*, and *month*.
- Put *length* away and get the word *half*.
- *Half* means that there are 2 equal parts. If I share half of my sandwich with you, I'll cut it down the middle. I won't get more than you, and you won't get more than me. Let's see if we can fold the strip of paper with the word *half* in half. (Demonstrate.)
- Point to the letter that makes the /h/ sound.
- Point to the letter that makes the /a/ sound.
- Point to the letter that makes the /f/ sound.
- Notice that one letter is silent. Which letter is that?
- Put *half* back with the other words. There are 6 words altogether. If we divide them in half, let's see if we can figure out how many words half would be.
- Let's collect our new words and save them to use later in the week.

Day 2: Word Whittle

Distribute the Lesson 28 words and have students place them across the top of their work space. Work through the following sets of clues as described on page 32.

First Word:

1. a word that has one vowel in it (*just, may, length, half*)
2. a word that has a letter that goes below the line (*just, may, length*)
3. a word that has four or fewer letters (*just, may*)
4. a word that rhymes with *must* (*just*)

Second Word:

1. a word that has at least 1 tall letter in it (*just, take, before, length, half*)
2. a word that has 2 tall letters (*take, before, length, half*)
3. a word that has 3 tall letters (*length, half*)
4. a word that refers to how long something is (*length*)

Third Word:

1. a word that has 4 letters (*just, take, half*)
2. a word that has a silent letter in it (*take, half*)

3. a word that starts with a tall letter (*take, half*)
4. a word that means "one of two equal parts of something" (*half*)

Fourth Word:
1. a word that has 1 syllable (*just, take, may, length, half*)
2. a word that has fewer than 5 letters (*just, take, may, half*)
3. a word that has an *a* in it (*may, take*)
4. a word that is also the name of a month (*may*)

Day 3: Free Choice Activity Day

Choose one or two of these activities (see pages 18–20):

- ☐ Word Match   ☐ Word Pop   ☐ Word Swat
- ☐ Word Sort   ☐ Voice Choice ☐ Cheer the Words
- ☐ Word Detective ☐ Rhymer   ☐ Other: _____

Word Sort

If you choose Word Sort, here are categories that fit this week's words:

- words with 3, 4, or 6 letters
- words with tall letters
- words with letters below the line
- words with long vowel sounds
- words with silent letters
- words with 1 or 2 syllables
- words that end with vowels

Day 4: Word Builder

Distribute the letter strip of the Lesson 28 Word Card to each student. Have students separate the letters, reviewing the letter names as they place them in alphabetical order: *a, e, g, i, m, n, r, s,* and *u*.

Have students spell words as you call them out and write them on the board:

sun	mug	same	rain
run	snug	name	main
gun	smug	ring	gain
rug	game	sing	measuring

On the board or in a pocket chart, sort the written words according to the spelling patterns below.

-un	-ug	-ame	-ing	-ain
sun	rug	game	ring	rain
run	mug	same	sing	main
gun	snug	name		gain
	smug			

After you've sorted the words, have students read over the words in each column. Focus on the *-ame* words. Tell students that if they know this pattern, it can help them spell many other words. Invite students to brainstorm a list of other words that rhyme with *game*, recording them on the board: *came, dame, fame, lame, name, same, tame, blame, frame, shame.*

Day 5: Word Smart

Distribute the Lesson 28 words, and ask students to arrange them across the top of their desks, leaving work space below.

Ask students to respond to your questions by picking up the correct word(s) and holding it so that you can see their answers. *Can you find . . .*

- a word that rhymes with *shake*?
- a word that means "the measure of how long something is"?
- a word that has 2 syllables?
- a word that is a polite word?
- a word that starts with the same sound as *jacket*?
- a word that rhymes with *must*?
- a word that has the little word *us* in it?
- a word that has a silent *l* in it?
- a word that rhymes with *more*?
- a word that means "one of two equal parts"?
- a word that rhymes with *rust*?
- a word that has the /th/ sound in it?
- a word that starts with a /b/ sound?
- a word that starts with the same sound as *tool*?
- a word that ends with the /t/ sound?
- a word that starts with the same sound as *lake*?
- a word that rhymes with *way*?
- a word that rhymes with *rake*?
- a word that starts with the same sound as *happy*?
- a word that has 3 vowels in it?
- a word that ends with the sound that *throw* starts with?
- a word that fits this sentence: "_____ I help you?"

✳ Homework ✳

Send the letters and words home with each student. Parents can use the words as flash cards and the letters to practice making words, as described in the Parent-Child Word Work sheet.

Day 1: Meet the Words

Pass out the Lesson 29 Word Cards, prepared as described on pages 14–15. Have students break apart the 6 new words and spread them on their desks. Ask students to do the following:

- Hold up each card as you pronounce the word on it.
- Look at the word, read it aloud, and spell it with you.
- Return the word card to the top of their desk.

Then guide students through the following activities, saying:

- Put the word *out* in your work space.
- What is the opposite of *out*?
  - Put your finger under the first 2 letters. They aren't very happy! They're making the /ou/ sound, as if they're hurt! Sometimes *o-u* makes that sound, and sometimes *o-w* makes that same sound.
  - What word would we have if we put a *p* at the beginning? An *s-h*? An *s-c*? The *-out* spelling pattern can help us spell other words.
  - Put *out* back and get the word that starts with the same letter as *out*. (old)
  - What is the opposite of *old*?
  - Point to the first letter. It makes a long-*o* sound that says its own letter name–/ō/.
  - Point to the letters as I make their sounds: /l/, /d/.
  - What word would we have if we put a *g* at the beginning? An *m*? A *b*? A *c*? The *-old* spelling pattern can help us spell lots of other words.
- Put *old* back and get the word *going*.
- Point to the letter making the /g/ sound at the beginning.
- Put your finger on the letter that's saying its name, /ō/.
- Put your finger over the last 3 letters. What little word do we have?
- Put your finger over the first 2 letters. Now we have the *-ing* pattern. Many times we'll see verbs like *run, jump, come, go*, and *make* change by putting an *-ing* on the end. (Write these words in their *-ing* form on the board.)
- Let's put *going* back and get the word *always*.
- *Always* means "forever" or "every time." If I say that we will always go to lunch at 11 a.m., that means we will do that each and every day at that time.
- Cover the last 4 letters. Now we have a-l that says /al/. This is not the word *all*, though, because *all* is spelled with 2 *l*'s.

| out |
| old |
| going |
| always |
| country |
| continent |

- Cover the first 2 letters with your hand. Now we have the word *ways*. I might say, "There are 2 ways we can get to the office."
- Answer these questions with the words *always, sometimes, never*:
  - I eat ice cream for breakfast!
  - It's a sunny day.
  - We read every day in school.
  - We write every day in school.
  - School is open.
  - It gets dark at night.
- *Always* has 2 syllables. Let's clap them. *Al-ways*.
- Let's put *always* back and get the word *country*.
- Our country is the United States. It is made up of 50 states. Our state is _____. Our country has a president that is elected by the people to make decisions to help the states. (Show map if possible.)
- Some other countries are Mexico, Canada, France, Germany, and Italy. (Point out on the map.) Some countries don't have presidents. They may have prime ministers or kings.
- Put your finger under the letter that makes the /k/ sound. Notice that it's a *c* and not a *k*.
- Put your finger under the letter that makes the long-*e* sound at the end. Notice that it's a *y* and not an *e*. *Y* often makes the long-*e* sound when it's at the end.
- Let's put *country* back and get the big word *continent*.
- A continent is the largest type of landmass. Let's see what we mean by a large landmass. (Show map.) We live on the North American continent. (Outline this on a map.) Do you see that North America is nearly surrounded by water? North America has several countries in it–Canada, the United States, and Mexico. (You may wish to point out the 7 continents.)
- This word has 3 syllables. Let's clap them–*con-ti-nent*.
- Let's collect our new words and save them to use later in the week.

Day 2: Word Whittle

Distribute the Lesson 29 words and have students place them across the top of their work space. Work through the following sets of clues as described on page 32.

First Word:

1. a word that has the vowel *o* in it (*out, old, going, continent, country*)
2. a word that has a tall letter in it (*out, old, continent, country*)
3. a word that has 2 tall letters in it (*old, continent*)
4. a word that means "the largest type of landmass on Earth" (*continent*)

Second Word:

1. a word that has more than 1 syllable (*going, continent, country, always*)
2. a word that has a tall letter (*continent, country, always*)
3. a word that has something to do with land (*continent, country*)
4. ours is the United States (*country*)

Third Word:

1. a word that starts with a vowel (*out, old, always*)
2. a word that doesn't have 2 vowels together (*old, always*)
3. a word that has *l* as its second letter (*old, always*)
4. a word that means "each and every time" (*always*)

Fourth Word

1. a word that has two or more vowels (*out, going, continent, always, country*)
2. a word that begins with a consonant (*going, continent, country*)
3. a word that with the vowel *i* in it (*going, continent*)
4. a word that starts and ends with the same letter (*going*)

Day 3: Free Choice Activity Day

Choose one or two of these activities (see pages 18–20):

- ☐ Word Match
- ☐ Word Pop
- ☐ Word Swat
- ☐ Word Sort
- ☐ Voice Choice
- ☐ Cheer the Words
- ☐ Word Detective
- ☐ Rhymer
- ☐ Other: _____

Word Sort

If you choose Word Sort, here are categories that fit this week's words:

- words with 3 letters
- words with tall letters
- words with letters below the line
- words with long vowel sounds
- words with 1, 2, or 3 syllables
- words that relate to land
- words that start with *o*

Day 4: Word Builder

Distribute the letter strip of the Lesson 29 Word Card to each student. Have students separate the letters, reviewing the letter names as they place them in alphabetical order: *c, e, i, n, n, n, o, s, t,* and *t*.

Have students spell words as you call them out and write them on the board:

in	not	sent	test	continent
tin	cot	tent	contest	continents
sin	cent	nest		

On the board or in a pocket chart, sort the written words according to the spelling patterns below.

-in	-ot	-ent	-est
tin	not	sent	nest
sin	cot	tent	test
		continent	contest

After you've sorted the words, have students read over the words in each column. Focus on the *-ent* words. Tell students that if they know this pattern, it can help them spell many other words. Invite students to brainstorm a list of other words that rhyme with *sent*, recording them on the board: *bent, cent, dent, lent, rent, tent, vent, went.*

You may want to point out that rimes can help students read and write multisyllabic words as well. For instance, *invent, indent, decent,* and *recent* all contain the *-ent* pattern.

Day 5: Word Smart

Distribute the Lesson 29 words, and ask students to arrange them across the top of their desks, leaving work space below.

Ask students to respond to your questions by picking up the correct word(s) and holding it so that you can see their answers. *Can you find . . .*

- a word that starts with a vowel?
- a word that rhymes with *sold*? *shout*?
- a word that is the opposite of *coming*?
- a word that is the opposite of *young*?
- a word that has 3 syllables? 2 syllables? 1 syllable?
- a word that is the opposite of *in*?
- a word that is hiding the little word *try*? *way*? *go*?
- a word that starts with the /ou/ sound?
- a word that describes the United States of America?
- a word that describes North America?
- a word that means each and every time?
- a word that is the opposite of *never*?
- a word that ends with the /z/ sound?
- a word that starts with the same sound as the word *over*?
- a word that has the same ending pattern as the word *running*?
- a word that ends with a /t/ sound?

❋ Homework ❋

Send the letters and words home with each student. Parents can use the words as flash cards and the letters to practice making words, as described in the Parent-Child Word Work sheet.

Day 1: Meet the Words

Pass out the Lesson 30 Word Cards, prepared as described on pages 14–15. Have students break apart the 6 new words and spread them on their desks. Ask students to do the following:

- Hold up each card as you pronounce the word on it.
- Look at the word, read it aloud, and spell it with you.
- Return the word card to the top of their desk.

Then guide students through the following activities, saying:

- Put the word *every* in your work space.
- This word has 2 syllables. Let's clap them.

every

again

very

predict

information

vowel

- Put your finger under the letter that makes the /v/ sound.
- Cover the first letter with your finger. What word do we have hiding there?
- Put your finger on the letter that makes the long-*e* sound at the end. *Y* is making that sound.
- I might use *every* in the sentence, "Every word we're meeting today is important to us." That means all of these words.
- Put *every* back and get *again*.
- *Again* means "once more." "Can we sing that song again?"
- This word has 2 syllables. Let's clap them.

- Cover the first 3 letters with your hand. What little word is hiding there?
- Put *again* back and get the word *very*.
- In which of our other words did we see this word hiding? (*every*)
- We use *very* to mean "extremely" or to stress something—"It's very hot today." Or "I'm very tired."
- This little word has 2 syllables. Let's clap them.
- Point to the letter that makes the long-*e* sound. It's not the *e*, is it? It's the *y*.
- Put *very* back and get *predict*.
- *Predict* means "to guess at what may happen." Before we read, we predict what we'll be reading about.
- *Predict* has 2 syllables. Let's clap them.
- Cover the last 4 letters with your hand. This word part *pre* has its own meaning. It means "before." If we have a pre-test, it's the little test we take before the real test to see how much we need

to study. We might preview a movie, which lets us see short clips before we spend our money to see the whole movie.

- Put *predict* back and get the big word *information*.
- Information is the knowledge we get or facts we learn in what we study. (Give an example of information the class gained from something studied recently.)
- This word has 4 syllables. Let's clap them.
- Now cover the last 5 letters. We have the word *inform*. *Inform* means to give information or news. "The president informs us about what is happening in our country."
- Put *information* back and get the word *vowel*.
- Every syllable in every word has at least 1 vowel. The vowels are: *a, e, i, o, u,* and sometimes *y* when it "acts" like an *i*.
- Words are made up of consonants and vowels. There are 2 words that are made up of only 1 vowel. Do you know what they are? (*I* and *a*)
- *Vowel* has 2 syllables. Let's clap them.
- Cover the last 2 letters with your finger. Now we have the little word *vow* which means "to make a promise."
- Do you hear the "hurt sound" after the *v–*/ou/?
- Let's collect our new words and save them to use later in the week.

Day 2: Word Whittle

Distribute the Lesson 30 words and have students place them across the top of their work space. Work through the following sets of clues as described on page 32.

First Word:

1. a word that has 2 or more syllables (*every, again, very, predict, vowel*)
2. a word that has a letter that goes below the line (*every, again, very, predict*)
3. a word that has 2 of the same letters (*every, again*)
4. a word that has the little word *very* in it (*every*)

Second Word:

1. a word that starts with a vowel (*every, again, information*)
2. a word that ends with an *n* (*again, information*)
3. a word that has the little word *in* inside (*again, information*)
4. a word that has 4 syllables (*information*)

Third Word:

1. a word that has more than four letters (*every, information, predict, vowel, again*)
2. a word that starts with a vowel (*every, information, again*)

3. a word that has 2 of the same vowel (*every, again*)
4. a word that ends with the same sound *no* starts with (*again*)

Fourth Word:

1. a word that has an *e* in it (*every, very, predict, vowel*)
2. a word that has no tall letters (*every, very*)
3. a word that rhymes with *towel* (*vowel*)

Day 3: Free Choice Activity Day

Choose one or two of these activities (see pages 18–20):

☐ Word Match   ☐ Word Pop   ☐ Word Swat

☐ Word Sort   ☐ Voice Choice   ☐ Cheer the Words

☐ Word Detective   ☐ Rhymer   ☐ Other: _____

Word Sort

If you choose Word Sort, here are categories that fit this week's words:

- words with 5 letters
- words with tall letters
- words with letters below the line
- words with 2 or 3 syllables
- words that start with vowels

Day 4: Word Builder

Distribute the letter strip of the Lesson 30 Word Card to each student. Have students separate the letters, reviewing the letter names as they place them in alphabetical order: *a, f, i, i, m, n, n, o, o, r,* and *t.*

Have students spell words as you call them out and write them on the board:

in	moon	arm	form
fin	noon	farm	inform
tin		far	information
		tar	

On the board or in a pocket chart, sort the written words according to the spelling patterns shown below.

-in	-oon	-arm	-ar
fin	moon	farm	tar
tin	noon		far

After you've sorted the words, have students read over the words in each column.

Focus on the *-oon* words. Tell students that if they know this pattern, it can help them spell many other words. Point out that another pattern represents the same sound, *-une.* Invite students to brainstorm a list of other words that rhyme with *moon,* recording them on the board by their spelling pattern: *boon, coon, goon, loon, noon, soon, dune, June, rune, tune.*

You may want to point out that rimes can help students read and write multisyllabic words as well. For instance, *lagoon, raccoon, pontoon,* and *maroon* all contain the *-oon* pattern.

Day 5: Word Smart

Distribute the Lesson 30 words, and ask students to arrange them across the top of their desks, leaving work space below.

Ask students to respond to your questions by picking up the correct word(s) and holding it so that you can see their answers.
Can you find . . .

- a word that starts with a vowel?
- a word that starts with the /p/ sound?
- a word that has 4 syllables?
- a word that rhymes with *merry*?
- a word that rhymes with *towel*?
- a word that fits in this sentence: "We were _____ tired after swimming all day"?
- a word that has 3 syllables?
- a word that has 2 syllables?
- a word that is hiding one of our words from this week? (*every*)
- a word that is hiding the word *in*?
- a word that starts with the same sound as the word *valley*?
- a word that names something that every syllable has?
- a word that names something you would find in a book of nonfiction?
- a word that means *a, e, i, o, u* and sometimes *y*?
- a word that starts with a vowel?
- a word hiding the word *inform*?
- a word that starts with a little word part that means *before*?

❄ Homework ❄

Send the letters and words home with each student. Parents can use the words as flash cards and the letters to practice making words, as described in the Parent-Child Word Work sheet.

Day 1: Meet the Words

Pass out the Lesson 31 Word Cards, prepared as described on pages 14–15. Have students break apart the 6 new words and spread them on their desks. Ask students to do the following:

- Hold up each card as you pronounce the word on it.
- Look at the word, read it aloud, and spell it with you.
- Return the word card to the top of their desk.

Then guide students through the following activities, saying:

- Put the word *walk* in your work space.
- This word can be an action verb that means to move around on foot, or it can be a noun that means a path.

walk

give

which

invent

matter

classify

- Point to the letter that makes the /w/ sound. What word would we have if we put a *t* in its place? A *c-h* in its place? Remember that *-alk* will help you spell those words.
- Put the word *walk* back and get *give*.
- *Give* usually means "to hand something to someone or present them with something." I want you to give your word *give* to one of your buddies. Now, buddies, give the word back to the person who gave it to you.
- Point to the letters that make these sounds—/g/, /i/, /v/.
- Cover the first letter and say the remainder of the word *-ive*. What word would we have if we put an *l* in front?
- Put *give* back and get the word *which*.
- I might use *which* to ask a question, "Which day do you want to go to the movies?" It tells you there's a choice to be made.
- This word starts with 2 buddy letters that together say /hw/ as in *what*.
- We have 2 more buddy letters in this word that together represent the sound /ch/. Point to those letters.
- The word *church* (write it) starts and ends with the /ch/ sound. (Say the sound as you underline the *c-h* in the word you've written.)
- Put the word *which* back and get the word *invent*. This is the first of 3 science words this week.
- *Invent* means "to create something, usually something useful, that has never been made before." Thomas Edison invented the light bulb. Alexander Graham Bell invented the telephone.
- Someone who invents something is called an *inventor*. (Write this on the board.)

- If you could invent something, what would it be? (Call on several to share or have them share with buddies.)
- *Invent* has 2 syllables. Let's clap them.
- Point to the letter that makes the /v/ sound.
- Point to the last letter, which makes the /t/ sound.
- Put *invent* back and get *matter*.
- In science, *matter* is any object or substance that can be touched or seen—anything solid, like a pencil, a shoe, a tree; anything liquid, like water, fuel, or lemonade. All matter is made of tiny molecules.
- *Matter* has other definitions too. For instance, I might say, "Does this matter to you?" That *matter* means "to have importance."
- This word has 2 syllables. Let's clap them.
- Cover the last 3 letters, and you'll see the little word *mat*.
- The last two letters are *e* and *r*. Together, they represent the /er/ sound.
- Put *matter* back and get *classify*.
- *Classify* means "to group things that are alike." In science, we learn to classify animals. Birds are one class; amphibians are another one, in which there are frogs; reptiles are a class in which there are crocodiles; insects are another class. There are many classifications. When we classify, we sort and look for like things.
- We classify or sort our words by the ways they are alike.
- This word has 3 syllables. Let's clap them.
- Listen to the ending of this word, which makes the long-*i* sound. The *y* is making that sound.
- Let's collect our new words and save them to use later in the week.

Day 2: Word Whittle

Distribute the Lesson 31 words and have students place them across the top of their work space. Work through the following sets of clues as described on page 32.

First Word:
1. a word that has more than four letters (*classify, which, invent, matter*)
2. a word that has an *i* in it (*classify, which, invent*)
3. a word that starts with two consonants in a row (*classify, which*)
4. a word that starts with a /hw/ sound (*which*)

Second Word:
1. a word that has a tall letter (*walk, which, invent, matter, classify*)
2. a word that has 2 tall letters (*walk, which, matter, classify*)
3. a word that has more than 1 syllable (*matter, classify*)
4. a word that means "to put together things that are alike" (*classify*)

Third Word:

1. a word that has the vowel *i* in it (*give, which, invent, classify*)
2. a word that has more than one vowel (*give, invent, classify*)
3. a word that starts with a consonant (*give, classify*)
4. a word that rhymes with the verb *live* (*give*)

Fourth Word:

1. a word that has the vowel *a* in it (*walk, matter, classify*)
2. a word that has 2 tall letters (*walk, matter, classify*)
3. a word that does not have a letter that extends below the line (*walk, matter*)
4. a word that rhymes with *talk* (*walk*)

Day 3: Free Choice Activity Day

Choose one or two of these activities (see pages 18–20):

☐ Word Match   ☐ Word Pop   ☐ Word Swat

☐ Word Sort   ☐ Voice Choice   ☐ Cheer the Words

☐ Word Detective   ☐ Rhymer   ☐ Other: _____

Word Sort

If you choose Word Sort, here are categories that fit this week's words:

- words with 4, 5, or 6 letters
- words with tall letters
- words with letters below the line
- words with 1, 2, or 3 syllables

Day 4: Word Builder

Distribute the letter strip of the Lesson 31 Word Card to each student. Have students separate the letters, reviewing the letter names as they place them in alphabetical order: *e, i, i, n, n, n, o, t, v,* and *s.*

Have students spell words as you call them out and write them on the board:

vine	ten	vet	invent
nine	tens	vets	inventions
nest	tennis	sent	
vest	vote	vent	

On the board or in a pocket chart, sort the written words according to the spelling patterns below.

-ine	-est	-ent
nine	nest	sent
vine	vest	vent

After you've sorted the words, have students read over the words in each column. Focus on the *-ine* words. Tell students that if they know this pattern, it can help them spell many other words. Invite students to brainstorm a list of other words that rhyme with *nine,* recording them on the board: *dine, fine, line, mine, pine, tine, vine, wine, brine, shine, twine.* You may want to point out that rimes can help students read and write multisyllabic words as well. For instance, *divine, entwine, sunshine,* and *refine* all contain the *-ine* pattern.

Take the opportunity to talk more about various inventions and forms of the word: invent, invention, and inventor.

Day 5: Word Smart

Distribute the Lesson 31 words, and ask students to arrange them across the top of their desks, leaving work space below.

Ask students to respond to your questions by picking up the correct word(s) and holding it so that you can see their answers. If there are more than 2 correct words, ask them to show only 2—one in each hand. Ask students, *Can you find . . .*

- a word that has 2 syllables?
- a word that rhymes with *chalk*? *splatter*?
- a word that fits in this sentence: "I would like to _____ a car that flies"?
- a word that has 3 syllables?
- a word that is hiding the little word *in*? *vent*? *mat*?
- a word hiding the little word that means all of us together? (*class–classify*)
- a word that starts with the same sound as the word *water*?
- a word that names something that is made of tiny molecules and can be touched?
- a word that fits in this sentence: "_____ flavor of ice cream do you like best?"
- a word that rhymes with the verb *live*?
- a word that means sorting things?
- a word that fits in this sentence: "Please _____ me your homework before we begin our lesson"?
- a word that ends with the same sound as the word *switch.*
- a word that ends with a silent letter?
- a word that has a double consonant?

✳ Homework ✳

Send the letters and words home with each student. Parents can use the words as flash cards and the letters to practice making words, as described in the Parent-Child Word Work sheet.

Day 1: Meet the Words

Pass out the Lesson 32 Word Cards, prepared as described on pages 14–15. Have students break apart the 6 new words and spread them on their desks. Ask students to do the following:

- Hold up each card as you pronounce the word on it.
- Look at the word, read it aloud, and spell it with you.
- Return the word card to the top of their desk.

Then guide students through the following activities, saying:

- Put the word *round* in your work space.
- Take the word *round* and go find something in the room that has a round shape. (Call on several to share.)
  - Point to the letter that makes the /r/ sound.
  - Put your finger under the next 2 letters that make the /ou/ sound that hurts.
  - Put your finger over the *r*. What word would we have if we put as *s* in its place? An *m* in its place? A *b*? Remember that *-ound* will help you spell those words.
  - Put the word *round* back and get *live*.
  - This is a very unusual word. It can be pronounced /liv/ to mean something that has life. I might say, "We water plants so that they can live." Or it can mean where your home is, as in, "I live on Maple Street." This *live* rhymes with *give*. But, *l-i-v-e* can also be pronounced with a long-*i*

round

live

fast

fantasy

reality

fiction

sound, /līv/. This word means something you are viewing is happening as you watch it and is not recorded. I might say, "This TV show is live."

- Put *live* back and get the word *fast*.
- *Fast* means moving very quickly. When you race, you run as fast as you can!
- Put your finger on the letter that makes the /f/ sound.
- Now cover the *f* with your finger. If we said /m/ instead of /f/, what word would we have? What about /bl/?
- This word has one syllable. Let's clap it: *fast*.
- Put the word *fast* back and get the word *fantasy*. This is the first of 3 language arts words this week. These are words that we'll use when we read some of our stories.
- *Fantasy* is a type of story that comes from the imagination of the author. It's not real. It may have characters that can do things that don't happen in the real world. Many fantasy stories have kings,

queens, and other royalty. Fairy tales can be classified as fantasy. What happened in the story of Cinderella that couldn't really have happened? That's what makes it fantasy.

- This word has 3 syllables. Let's clap it: *fan-ta-sy*.
- What letter is making the long-*e* sound at the end?
- Let's put *fantasy* back and get *reality*.
- Put your finger over the last 3 letters. Now we have the word *real*. That word will help us remember what this word means. *Reality* means that something is taken from real life. In stories of reality, we wouldn't have superheroes, flying horses, or talking animals. The story may not be true, but it could happen.
- This word has 4 syllables. Let's clap them: *re-al-i-ty*.
- We hear all of the letters in this word. Point to them as I pronounce the word slowly. (Say the word slowly.)
- Put the word *reality* back and get the word *fiction*.
- *Fiction* is another of our language arts words. *Fiction* is a kind of story that is not true. Fantasy like Cinderella is a kind of fiction. (Give examples of fiction that have been read in the class.)
- Put your finger on the letter making the /f/ sound, the short *i* sound /i/, and the /k/.
- Cover those first 3 letters. The *-tion* ending is pronounced /shun/. You'll see that ending on many words like *education, action, motion,* and *station*.
- Let's collect our new words and save them to use later in the week.

Day 2: Word Whittle

Distribute the Lesson 32 words and have students place them across the top of their work space. Work through the following sets of clues as described on page 32.

First Word:

1. a word that has more than 1 syllable (*fantasy, reality, fiction*)
2. a word that ends with a long-*e* sound (*fantasy, reality*)
3. a word that has a tall letter (*fantasy, reality*)
4. a word that means something is real (*reality*)

Second Word:

1. a word that has a tall letter (*round, live, fantasy, reality, fiction, fast*)
2. a word that starts with an *f* (*fantasy, fiction, fast*)
3. a word with more than 1 syllable (*fantasy, fiction*)
4. a word that has 2 syllables (*fiction*)

Third Word:

1. a word that has a *t* in it (*fast, fantasy, reality, fiction*)
2. a word that relates to stories (*fantasy, reality, fiction*)

3. a word that starts with the sound /f/ (*fantasy, fiction*)
4. a word that ends with the long-*e* sound (*fantasy*)

Fourth Word:

1. a word that has more than 4 letters (*round, fiction, reality, fantasy*)
2. a word that has two different vowels (*round, fiction, reality*)
3. a word that does not end with the long-*e* sound (*fiction, round*)
4. a word that names a shape (*round*)

Day 3: Free Choice Activity Day

Choose one or two of these activities (see pages 18–20):

- ☐ Word Match   ☐ Word Pop   ☐ Word Swat
- ☐ Word Sort   ☐ Voice Choice   ☐ Cheer the Words
- ☐ Word Detective   ☐ Rhymer   ☐ Other: _____

Word Sort

If you choose Word Sort, here are categories that fit this week's words:

- words with 4, 5, or 7 letters
- words with tall letters
- words with letters below the line
- words with 1, 2, 3, or 4 syllables
- words with *y* (long-*e*) endings
- words that relate to stories

Day 4: Word Builder

Distribute the letter strip of the Lesson 32 Word Card to each student. Have students separate the letters, reviewing the letter names as they place them in alphabetical order: *a, a, e, f, i, l, r, s, t,* and *y.*

Have students spell words as you call them out and write them on the board:

it	ray	relay	*reality*
fit	say	layer	*fair*
sit	stay	flat	*fairly*
set	lay	slat	*fairy*
yet			*fairy tales*

On the board or in a pocket chart, sort the written words according to the spelling patterns below.

-it	-et	-ay	-at
fit	set	lay	flat
sit	yet	ray	slat
		say	
		stay	

After you've sorted the words, have students read over the words in each column. Focus on the -*it* words. Tell students that if they know this pattern, it can help them spell many other words. Invite students to brainstorm a list of other words that rhyme with *fit*, recording them on the board: *bit, hit, kit, lit, pit, sit, wit, chit, grit, flit, knit, slit, split.* You may want to point out that rimes can help students read and write multisyllabic words as well. For instance, *admit, orbit, permit,* and *unfit* all contain the -*it* pattern.

Take the opportunity to talk about some of the word endings such as safe/safer/safely/safety and fair/fairly.

Day 5: Word Smart

Distribute the Lesson 32 words, and ask students to arrange them across the top of their desks, leaving work space below.

Ask students to respond to your questions by picking up the correct word(s) and holding it so that you can see their answers. *Can you find . . .*

- a word that has 2 syllables?
- a word that has 1 syllable?
- a word that has 4 syllables?
- a word that has the little word *fan* hiding inside?
- a word that rhymes with *give*?
- a word that rhymes with *past*?
- a word that rhymes with *hive*?
- a word that has the little word *it* inside?
- a word that has the little word *ant* inside?
- a word that means something is real?
- a word that means to move quickly?
- a word that means a story has things in it that can't happen in the real world?
- a word that rhymes with *found*?
- a word that fits in this sentence: "I know the story is _____ because it has fire-breathing dragons in it"?
- a word that ends with a long-*e* sound but doesn't end with an *e*?
- a word that starts with the same sound as the word *love*?
- a word that ends with the same sound as the word *wood*?
- a word that has the word *as* inside?
- a word that has the word *an* inside?

Day 1: Meet the Words

Pass out the Lesson 33 Word Cards, prepared as described on pages 14–15. Have students break apart the 6 new words and spread them on their desks. Ask students to do the following:

- Hold up each card as you pronounce the word on it.
- Look at the word, read it aloud, and spell it with you.
- Return the word card to the top of their desk.

Then guide students through the following activities, saying:

- Put the word *once* in your work space.
- *Once* means "one time." I might say, "I want you to write your name on the paper once." Also, many fairy tales start off with the words, "Once upon a time…"
- Put the word *once* back and get the word *your,* spelled *y-o-u-r.* (Be sure they choose the right word instead of *you're.*)
- *Your* means that something belongs to you—your hat or your book.
- Put your finger on the letter that makes the /y/ sound. Now cover the *y* with your finger. We now have the word *our,* which means something belongs to us—our classroom or our school.
- Get the word *you're* and put it below the word *your.*
- These words look very much alike and sound alike, but they have different meanings.
- Cover the final letter *e* in the word *you're.* Now both words have the same spelling, *y-o-u-r.* But, one word also has an apostrophe, which lets us know that a letter is missing. This word is a contraction. *You're* is the same as *you are,* but we use the apostrophe to show that the *a* is missing.
- I might use *you're* to say, "I know you're 6 years old."
- Use your hand to cover the apostrophe, *r,* and *e.* Now we have the word *you.*
- What letter does the apostrophe stand for in this word? If we had the *a, a-r-e* would spell *are.*
- Put these words back and get the word *greater.*
- We might use the word *greater* to compare the value of two objects or things. If we're talking about numbers, 6 is greater than 5, 10 is greater than 5. Which is greater: 2 or 4?
- Put your finger under the first two letters. These buddy letters represent the sound /gr/ when they're together.

once

your

you're

greater

vertical

horizontal

- Listen to the sound that comes after the /gr/: /ā/. The *e* and *a* together represent the long-*a* sound.
- The *e* and *r* work together to represent the /er/ sound. When we hear /er/, it's usually an *e-r, i-r,* or *u-r.*
- We add *e-r* to the word *great* when we want to compare two things, to show that something is better or bigger than another.
- Put *greater* back and get the word *vertical.*
- Put your elbows on your desk and lay your arm down flat. Now keep your elbow on the desk and raise your forearm straight up. Your arms are vertical to the desk—straight up and down. That's what vertical means—"straight up and down."
- This word has 3 syllables. Let's clap them: *ver-ti-cal.*
- Point to the letter that makes these sounds: /k/, /a/, /l/.
- Put your elbows on your desk again, and raise your forearms up straight again, so they're vertical. Now lower your arms to be flat on your desk. Your arms are now horizontal to the desk—flat, side to side.
- The sun rises and sets on the horizon—the line between the land and the sky. (Draw)
- Get the word *horizontal* from your pack of words. This word has 4 syllables. Let's clap them: *hor-i-zon-tal.*
- The ending of the word is just like the end part of *vertical*—*horizontal.*
- Let's practice telling the difference between vertical and horizontal. Put your elbows on your table. Show me horizontal and vertical with your forearms straight up or flat on the desk when I say vertical and horizontal. (Repeat these words and let students respond with their hands.)
- Let's collect our new words and save them to use later in the week.

Day 2: Word Whittle

Distribute the Lesson 33 words and have students place them across the top of their work space. Work through the following sets of clues as described on page 32.

First Word:
1. a word that ends with a consonant (*horizontal, vertical, greater, your*)
2. a word whose second letter is a vowel (*horizontal, vertical, your*)
3. a word that means "straight up and down" (*vertical*)

Second Word:
1. a word that has the vowel *o* in it (*once, your, you're, horizontal*)
2. a word that has no tall letters (*once, your, you're*)
3. a word that has the little word *on* in it (*once*)

Third Word:

1. a word that has more than four letters (*vertical, horizontal, greater, you're*)
2. a word that has a tall letter in it (*vertical, horizontal, greater*)
3. a word that means "side to side" like the line where the sky meets the earth (*horizontal*)

Fourth Word:

1. a word that has the vowel *e* in it (*once, you're, vertical, greater*)
2. A word that does not have an apostrophe (*once, vertical, greater*)
3. a word that means the larger of two items (*greater*)

Day 3: Free Choice Activity Day

Choose one or two of these activities (see pages 18–20):

- ☐ Word Match   ☐ Word Pop   ☐ Word Swat
- ☐ Word Sort   ☐ Voice Choice   ☐ Cheer the Words
- ☐ Word Detective   ☐ Rhymer   ☐ Other: _____

Word Sort

If you choose Word Sort, here are categories that fit this week's words:

- words with 4 letters
- words with tall letters
- words with letters below the line
- words with 1, 2, 3, or 4 syllables

Day 4: Word Builder

Distribute the letter strip of the Lesson 33 Word Card to each student. Have students separate the letters, reviewing the letter names as they place them in alphabetical order: *e, f, l, o, r, s, u,* and *y.*

Have students spell words as you call them out and write them on the board:

fly	self	fore	our	your
sly	or	lore	flour	yourself
elf	for	sore		

On the board or in a pocket chart, sort the written words according to the spelling patterns below.

-y	-elf	-ore	-our
fly	self	fore	our
sly	yourself	lore	flour
		sore	your*

* (note different pronunciation)

After you've sorted the words, have students read over the words in each column. Focus on the *-ore* words. Tell students that if they know this pattern, it can help them spell many other words. If students generate words that rhyme with *sore* but are spelled with a different pattern, just make a new column and tell them that sometimes the same sound can be represented by more than one letter pattern. It's also an opportunity to discuss homophones, such as *pore* and *poor*; *for, four,* and *fore*; and *sore* and *soar*. Invite students to brainstorm a list of other words that rhyme with *sore,* recording them on the board: *bore, core, fore, gore, lore, more, pore, tore, wore, chore, store, door, poor, floor, for, nor.* You may want to point out that rimes can help students read and write multisyllabic words as well. For instance, *adore, explore, galore, ignore,* and *restore* all contain the *-ore* pattern.

Day 5: Word Smart

Distribute the Lesson 33 words, and ask students to arrange them across the top of their desks, leaving work space below.

Ask students to respond to your questions by picking up the correct word(s) and holding it so that you can see their answers. *Can you find . . .*

- a word that has 2 syllables?
- a word that has 1 syllable?
- a word that has 3 syllables?
- a word that has 4 syllables?
- the longest word in this week's set?
- a word that is a contraction?
- a word that means "one time"?
- a word that describes something positioned straight side to side?
- a word that describes something positioned straight up and down?
- a word that refers to something that belongs to you?
- a word that starts the same way the word *horse* starts?
- a word that is hiding the little word that means "where the sky meets the earth"?
- a word that is hiding the little word *eat*? the word *on*?
- a word that fits in this sentence: "Ten is _____ than 8"?
- a word that starts with the same sound *green* starts with?

Day 1: Meet the Words

Pass out the Lesson 34 Word Cards, prepared as described on pages 14–15. Have students break apart the 6 new words and spread them on their desks. Ask students to do the following:

- Hold up each card as you pronounce the word on it.
- Look at the word, read it aloud, and spell it with you.
- Return the word card to the top of their desk.

Then guide students through the following activities, saying:

- Put the word *their* in your work space.
- *Their* means that something belongs to "them"–their house, their classroom.

their

put

enough

graph

chart

solve

- We've had another word that sounds just like this one–*there*. (Write it.) It has a different meaning. So, we'll have to keep these tricky words straight.
- This word has one syllable. Let's clap it: *their*.
- Point to the 2 letters that make the /th/ sound at the beginning.
- Put *their* back and get *put*.
- *Put* means "to place or set" something somewhere. *Put your shoes in your room.*
- Point to each letter as I make its sound: /p/, /u/, /t/.
- This word has one syllable: *put.*
- Put *put* back and get *enough*.

- I might say, "Have you had enough to eat?" Or, "I think we've had enough time to draw our pictures."
- This word has 2 syllables. Let's clap them: *e-nough*.
- Listen carefully to the ending sound, /f/. It sounds like there should be an *f* but 2 other letters are tricking us. The *g-h* together represent the /f/ sound.
- Put *enough* back and get *graph*.
- We use graphs to show data or information that has been collected. A graph uses a picture and some words to give this information. Let's make a graph on the board. (Sketch a graph on the board, labeling the y-axis 1-10 and the x-axis with types of pets. Ask students to raise their hand if they have a particular pet, and record the data on the graph.) This is a graph that represents the information we have gathered.
- Point to the first 2 letters that blend to make the /gr/ sound.
- Point to the letter that makes the /a/ sound.
- Listen to this word carefully. (Say it slowly.) What letters do you

think are making the /f/ sound, since there's no *f* in this word? In this word we have *p-h* to represent /f/; in *enough*, we had *g-h*.

- Put *graph* back and get *chart*.
- A chart is another way we can show information. (Show them some of the charts in your classroom.)
- Put your finger under the first 2 letters that represent the sound /ch/. This is the same way words like *chocolate*, *church*, *chicken*, and *chips* start.
- Cover the first 2 letters. What word do you see? Many times we use art to make a chart!
- Sometimes the words *chart* and *graph* are used for each other since they are a lot alike.
- Put *chart* back and get another math word–*solve*.
- When we solve a problem, we find answers or solutions. We have problems and solutions in our lives, and we have problems and solutions in math. In our classroom, if 2 of you want to use the same paintbrush, we would need to solve the problem by sharing. One of you could use it first and then give it to your friend when you're through. One math problem might be–What is 2 plus 2? We solve it by adding, and the solution is 4. We like to solve our life problems and our math problems!
- Point to the letter that makes these sounds: /s/, /o/, /l/, /v/.
- Let's collect our new words and save them to use later in the week.

Day 2: Word Whittle

Distribute the Lesson 34 words and have students place them across the top of their work space. Work through the following sets of clues as described on page 32.

First Word:
1. a word that has one syllable (*their, graph, chart, put, solve*)
2. a word that starts with two consonants in a row (*their, graph, chart*)
3. a word that has the vowel *a* in it (*graph, chart*)
4. a word that has an /f/ sound in it but no letter *f* (*graph*)

Second Word:
1. a word that has a tall letter in it (*their, put, graph, chart, solve*)
2. a word that has an *r* in it (*their, graph, chart*)
3. a word that has 2 tall letters (*their, chart*)
4. a word that rhymes with *smart* (*chart*)

Third Word:
1. a word that has 5 letters in it (*their, chart, graph, solve*)
2. a word that ends with a consonant (*their, chart, graph*)
3. a word that has 2 tall letters (*their, chart*)
4. a word that tell us something belongs to "them" (*their*)

Fourth Word:

1. a word that has two or more vowels (*enough, their, solve*)
2. a word that begins or ends with a vowel (*enough, solve*)
3. a word that means to find a solution or an answer (*solve*)

Day 3: Free Choice Activity Day

Choose one or two of these activities (see pages 18–20):

☐ Word Match   ☐ Word Pop   ☐ Word Swat

☐ Word Sort   ☐ Voice Choice   ☐ Cheer the Words

☐ Word Detective   ☐ Rhymer   ☐ Other: _____

Word Sort

If you choose Word Sort, here are categories that fit this week's words:

* words with 5 or 6 letters
* words with tall letters
* words with letters below the line
* words with 1 or 2 syllables
* words with the /f/ sound
* words that start with vowels or consonants
* words that start with blends

Day 4: Word Builder

Distribute the letter strip of the Lesson 34 Word Card to each student. Have students separate the letters, reviewing the letter names as they place them in alphabetical order: *a, g, h, h, o, o, p, p, r, s,* and *t*.

Have students spell words as you call them out and write them on the board:

pop	pot	spot	*graph*
top	got	port	*graphs*
hop	hot	sport	*photo*
stop	shot	sap	*photos*
		gap	*photographs*

On the board or in a pocket chart, sort the written words according to the spelling patterns below.

-op	-ot	-ort	-ap
pop	pot	port	sap
top	hot	sport	gap
hop	shot		
stop	spot		

After you've sorted the words, have students read over the words in each column.

Focus on the *-ap* words. Tell students that if they know this pattern, it can help them spell many other words. Invite students to brainstorm a list of other words that rhyme with *sap*, recording them on the board: *cap, gap, lap, map, nap, rap, tap, yap, zap, chap, clap, flap, scrap, slap, snap, strap, trap, wrap.*

You may want to point out that rimes can help students read and write multisyllabic words as well. For instance, *entrap, recap,* and *unwrap* all contain the *-ap* pattern.

Day 5: Word Smart

Distribute the Lesson 34 words, and ask students to arrange them across the top of their desks, leaving work space below.

Ask students to respond to your questions by picking up the correct word(s) and holding it so that you can see their answers.

Can you find . . .

* A word that starts with a vowel?
* A word that rhymes with *smart*?
* A word that starts with a /th/ sound?
* A word that has 2 of the same vowels?
* A word that means "to find an answer to a problem"?
* A word that starts with the /p/ sound?
* A word that is hiding the little word *art*?
* A word that is hiding the little word *rap*?
* A word that starts the same sound as the word *grey*?
* A word that ends with the same sound as *cough*?
* A word that relates to showing information?
* A word that rhymes with *mart*?
* A word that ends with a vowel?
* A word that ends with a silent letter?
* A word that has the /f/ sound but no letter *f*?
* A word with 2 syllables?
* A word that fits in this sentence: "Have you had _____ to eat?"

❋ Homework ❋

Send the letters and words home with each student. Parents can use the words as flash cards and the letters to practice making words, as described in the Parent-Child Word Work sheet.

Day 1: Meet the Words

Pass out the Lesson 35 Word Cards, prepared as described on pages 14–15. Have students break apart the 6 new words and spread them on their desks. Ask students to do the following:

- Hold up each card as you pronounce the word on it.
- Look at the word, read it aloud, and spell it with you.
- Return the word card to the top of their desk.

Then guide students through the following activities, saying:

- Put the word *because* in your work space.
- Cover the last 5 letters with your hand. The first 2 letters are the little word *be*.

| because |
| where |
| were |
| machine |
| environment |
| shelter |

- Cover the *b-e* and you'll find the word *cause*. I might say, "What was the cause of the accident?" Or, "What caused the ice to melt?"
- When we put *be* and *cause* together, this word tells us we're going to hear the reason for something. For example, I might say, "He won't be at school tomorrow because he is sick." Or, "We can't go outside and play because it is raining."
- Put *because* back and get the words *where* and *were*. Notice how much alike they are. What is the only letter they don't share? The *h* that they don't share makes a big difference. Listen carefully as I pronounce each word.
- Now, see if you can tell which word I'm saying. Pick up the word that says _____ (repeat *were* and *where* randomly and let students hold up the word they heard you pronounce).
- *Where* refers to a place. I might say, "Where do you live?"
- Turn to your buddy and ask them where they live and let them answer. Take turns asking and answering the question.
- *Were* is a verb that tells about something that has already happened. I might say, "Were you there when we read the book?" Or, "I know you were sick the day we read the book."
- Put those words back and get the word *machine*.
- A *machine* is a device that makes work easier. Let's see what machines we have in our classroom. (Show them the stapler, the computer, the pencil sharpener, etc.)
- Point to the letters that make these sounds: /m/ /a/.
- Point to the 2 buddy letters that make the sound /sh/. Often *c* and *h* together represent the sound /ch/, so this is a little tricky!

- This word has 2 syllables. Let's clap them: *ma-chine*.
- Put *machine* back and get the big word *environment*.
- *Environment* means "our surroundings, what is around us." We have a classroom environment, a school environment, a community environment, and a global environment.
- This word has 4 syllables. Let's clap them: *en-vi-ron-ment*.
- Now let's take our hands and cover up all the letters except for the ones in each syllable that we pronounce. (Say the letters just after you pronounce each syllable.)
- Put *environment* back and get *shelter*.
- A *shelter* is a structure that provides protection from the outdoors. If we're outside and it rains, we might run under a store awning that provides shelter. Even animals build shelters to protect themselves.
- Let's clap the 2 syllables: *shel-ter*.
- Point to the 2 buddy letters that represent /sh/.
- Point to the buddy letters *e-r* that represent /er/.
- Let's collect our new words and save them to use later in the week.

Day 2: Word Whittle

Distribute the Lesson 35 words and have students place them across the top of their work space. Work through the following sets of clues as described on page 32.

First Word:
1. a word that has the vowel *e* in it (*where, because, environment, were, machine, shelter*)
2. a word that has 2 *e*'s in it (*because, where, were, environment, shelter*)
3. a word that has 2 syllables (*because, shelter*)
4. a word that fits in this sentence: I am out of breath _____ I ran up the stairs. (*because*)

Second Word:
1. a word that ends with a vowel (*because, where, were, machine*)
2. a word that has a tall letter (*because, where, machine*)
3. a word that has an *h* in it (*where, machine*)
4. a word that starts with the /hw/ sound (*where*)

Third Word:
1. a word that has more than 1 syllable (*because, machine, environment, shelter*)
2. a word that starts with a consonant (*because, machine, shelter*)
3. a word that ends with a vowel (*because, machine*)
4. a word that ends with the same sound as the word *mine* (*machine*)

Fourth Word:

1. a word with two e's in it (*because, where, were, environment, shelter*)
2. a word that has a silent e on the end (*because, where, were*)
3. a word that starts with a w (*where, were*)
4. a word that rhymes with *there* (*where*)

Day 3: Free Choice Activity Day

Choose one or two of these activities (see pages 18–20):

- [ ] Word Match
- [ ] Word Pop
- [ ] Word Swat
- [ ] Word Sort
- [ ] Voice Choice
- [ ] Cheer the Words
- [ ] Word Detective
- [ ] Rhymer
- [ ] Other: _____

Word Sort

If you choose Word Sort, here are categories that fit this week's words:

- words with tall letters
- words with 1, 2, or 4 syllables
- words that start with *w*
- words that start with consonants
- words that end with vowels
- words with 2 of the same letter
- words that start with blends

Day 4: Word Builder

Distribute the letter strip of the Lesson 35 Word Card to each student. Have students separate the letters, reviewing the letter names as they place them in alphabetical order: *a, a, b, h, i, s, t,* and *t.*

Have students spell words as you call them out and write them on the board:

at	bat	sit	stab
hat	bath	hit	*habit*
that	it	bit	*habitat*
sat	its	tab	*habitats*

On the board or in a pocket chart, sort the written words according to the spelling patterns below.

-at	-it	-ab
hat	sit	tab
that	hit	stab
sat	bit	
bat		
habitat		

After you've sorted the words, have students read over the words in each column. Focus on the *-ab* words. Tell students that if they know this pattern, it can help them spell many other words. Invite students to brainstorm a list of other words that rhyme with *tab,* recording them on the board: *cab, dab, gab, jab, lab, nab, blab, crab, drab, grab, scab, slab, stab.* You may want to point out that rimes can help students read and write multisyllabic words as well. For instance, *habitat* has *-ab* as part of its first syllable.

Day 5: Word Smart

Distribute the Lesson 35 words, and ask students to arrange them across the top of their desks, leaving work space below.

Ask students to respond to your questions by picking up the correct word(s) and holding it so that you can see their answers. *Can you find . . .*

- a word that has 4 syllables?
- the word that is the shortest in this week's set?
- a word that rhymes with *there*?
- a word that is hiding the little word *in*?
- a word that is hiding the word *be*?
- a word that is hiding the word *he*?
- a word that refers to our surroundings—what's around us?
- a word hiding the little word *here*?
- a word hiding the little word *we*?
- a word that starts with the /hw/ sound?
- a word that starts with the /b/ sound?
- a word that starts with the /sh/ sound?
- a word that has 2 syllables?
- a word that has 1 syllable?
- a word that starts with the same sound as the word *white*?
- a word that has the same last syllable as *government*?
- a word with the sound /sh/ in the middle?

❋ Homework ❋

Send the letters and words home with each student. Parents can use the words as flash cards and the letters to practice making words, as described in the Parent-Child Word Work sheet.

am	me
an	name
man	same

a   e   m   n   s

 Systematic Word Study for Grade 1 © 2011 by Cheryl M. Sigmon, Scholastic Teaching Resources • Lesson 1

in	king
win	walk
wing	walking

a	g	i	k	l	n	w

at

met

sat

tall

let

small

a e l l l m s s t

Systematic Word Study for Grade 1 © 2011 by Cheryl M. Sigmon, Scholastic Teaching Resources • Lesson 3

in

tan

pin

pan

tap

paint

a   i   n   p   t

is

set

it

rest

get

tiger

e   i   g   r   s   t

they

pretty

please

went

saw

want

e   n   p   s   t

jump

after

who

well

help

our

a e f n n o o r t

Systematic Word Study for Grade 1 © 2011 by Cheryl M. Sigmon, Scholastic Teaching Resources • Lesson 7

brown

get

not

good

what

there

d e o p s t t

thank

had

some

his

stop

her

a f h k l n t u

Systematic Word Study for Grade 1 © 2011 by Cheryl M. Sigmon, Scholastic Teaching Resources • Lesson 9

under

must

black

say

white

soon

d e h n r t u

down

that

where

out

funny

into

c　e　i　n　s　s　t

Systematic Word Study for Grade 1 © 2011 by Cheryl M. Sigmon, Scholastic Teaching Resources • Lesson 11

said	state
city	little
citizen	play

a a e l m p t y

then	month
when	minute
I	total

e   i   m   n   s   t   u

you	look
too	how
red	year

a a c d e l n r

we

down

for

come

can't

light

c e m o p r t u

Systematic Word Study for Grade 1 © 2011 by Cheryl M. Sigmon, Scholastic Teaching Resources • Lesson 15

up

yellow

see

on

my

question

e i n o q s s t u

go

big

do

plant

one

planet

a   d   e   g   n   r   s

Systematic Word Study for Grade 1 © 2011 by Cheryl M. Sigmon, Scholastic Teaching Resources • Lesson 17

make

here

away

think

blue

unit

e c i p r s t u

run

from

find

skip

three

odd

a d e g i n r

but	has
with	again
this	future

a d h r s t u y

will

no

did

election

so

vote

c e e i l n o s t

Systematic Word Study for Grade 1 © 2011 by Cheryl M. Sigmon, Scholastic Teaching Resources • Lesson 21

like

me

yes

fly

four

weather

a a a e e h m n r t w

now

ran

new

past

to

present

a a d r s t u y

Systematic Word Study for Grade 1 © 2011 by Cheryl M. Sigmon, Scholastic Teaching Resources • Lesson 23

eat

could

ate

heat

him

freezing

a d d e e n s w y

of

open

much

hero

ask

honor

a e e n r s t v

Systematic Word Study for Grade 1 © 2011 by Cheryl M. Sigmon, Scholastic Teaching Resources • Lesson 25

as

would

them

character

many

setting

a a c c e h r r s t

over

don't

any

insect

know

cycle

a e g h o p p p r r s s

Systematic Word Study for Grade 1 © 2011 by Cheryl M. Sigmon, Scholastic Teaching Resources • Lesson 27

just	before
take	length
may	half

a e g i m n r s u

out

always

old

country

going

continent

c e i n n n o s t t

Systematic Word Study for Grade 1 © 2011 by Cheryl M. Sigmon, Scholastic Teaching Resources • Lesson 29

every	predict
again	information
very	vowel

a f i i m n n o o r t

walk

invent

give

matter

which

classify

e i i i n n n o t v s

Systematic Word Study for Grade 1 © 2011 by Cheryl M. Sigmon, Scholastic Teaching Resources • Lesson 31

round

fantasy

live

reality

fast

fiction

a a e f i l r s t y

once	greater
your	vertical
you're	horizontal

e f l o r s u y

Systematic Word Study for Grade 1 © 2011 by Cheryl M. Sigmon, Scholastic Teaching Resources • Lesson 33

their

graph

put

chart

enough

solve

a g h h o o p p r s t

because

machine

where

environment

were

shelter

a a b h i s t t

Systematic Word Study for Grade 1 © 2011 by Cheryl M. Sigmon, Scholastic Teaching Resources • Lesson 35

Dear Parents,

Every day in our class, we have a special time for word study. As students enjoy these fun activities, they will be growing in literacy through a systematic study of phonics, print and language concepts, and vocabulary. My belief is that this emphasis on words will make a positive difference in your child's ability to read and write and in his or her general achievement.

Every week, your child will bring home a sealed plastic bag with words and letters that we have used in our activities, along with a one-page homework sheet. I ask that you please find some time to work together with your child to complete this sheet.

Here are some directions for completing this homework:

- Use the single letter tiles to make different words. You may use all or some of the letters to construct six or more words. Your child will have done this during the week.

- The homework sheet includes a checklist to guide what you should expect your child to do with the words—discuss word features, spell many of the words, read the words accurately, and make new words with spelling patterns they have learned.

- Each week, there will be words listed as "special," and the checklist will ask that you discuss these with your child. You might talk about their meanings, where you might see or hear those words, and sentences that might use those words. If you notice those words in your daily life (signs, newspaper headlines, books, etc.), please point them out.

- The last portion of the sheet asks that you help your child make new words with spelling patterns that we have studied during the week. Your child will understand how this works. For example, if we have studied the –at pattern, the words *mat, cat, rat,* and *bat* can be made. When your child learns spelling patterns, he or she will be able to spell many new words.

- The last box you will check on the worksheet will be your confirmation that your child got "word power" that week. Your time and my time spent on words will surely have a big payoff for your child!

If you have questions, please let me know. Thank you for being my partner in the literacy growth of your child this year!

Sincerely,

Student Name _____ Date _____

Parent-Child Word Work

These are words we made with the **letters** from this week:

_____   _____

_____   _____

_____   _____

Parent: Please review your child's work. Place a ✓ or an ✗ in each box.

☐ My child was able to *tell* me some features of each **word** in the packet. (For example: sounds it has, how many tall letters or letters below the line, how many syllables/claps, little words hiding inside, etc.)

☐ My child was able to *use* each of the 6 words from the packet in a sentence.

☐ My child was able to *read* each of the 6 words in the packet.

☐ My child was able to *spell* each of the 6 words.
(*Note to Parent*: Please do not worry about correct spellings of big words that have more than 2 syllables. The meanings of these words are more important than the spellings at this grade level.)

☐ * We talked about this week's special words:

_____   _____

_____   _____

(*Note*: Please do not worry about the correct spelling of words with more than two syllables. At this grade level, knowing the meanings of these words is far more important.)

☐ * My child was able to make these new words with these spelling patterns: _____ , _____ :
(Example: -est = *best, vest, nest, test*)

_____ : _____

_____ : _____

_____ : _____

* *Words to be inserted by teacher.*

My child got word power this week!

Parent signature _____ Date _____

Systematic Word Study for Grade 1 © 2011 by Cheryl M. Sigmon, Scholastic Teaching Resources